Open the Doors!

Reginald and Barbara Olson

Reginald D. Olson, Publisher

Published and distributed by
Reginald D. and Barbara L. Olson
P.O. Box 317761
Cincinnati, Ohio 45231-7761

Library of Congress Cataloging in Publication Data
Open the doors/Reginald D. Olson
and Barbara L. Olson

ISBN 0-9653403-3-3

TABLE OF CONTENTS

PREFACE

In the year 2000 a major Protestant denomination adopted a new motto. It was "Open Hearts, Open Minds, Open Doors." Many church members thought the purpose of this new statement was to make the church more appealing to the public as it attempted to gain new members and balance its historical trend of declining membership.[1.] *

While many church members were happy to hear of this new image for our church some wondered if it were merely "window dressing" and not a realistic statement of the denomination's practices. Their concerns were based on the fact that the denomination's official stance toward the ordination and marriage of homosexual persons remained one of exclusion. Proponents for denominational inclusiveness had used the theme "open doors" at previous conferences to urge the church to accept homosexuals, seemingly to no avail. The denomination's motto seemed to be a reworking of the title of a journal called "*Open Hands*." This was the official vehicle of the support group for the GLBTX** community of several mainline denominations. Some annual conferences also began designating certain churches as "Welcoming Congregations" but required no particular commitment to serving GLBTX persons.

It seemed therefore that the new motto was "false advertising." This might backfire if GLBTX persons attempt to affiliate with a church whose doors are relatively closed to them.

Unfortunately, the doors of the churches seem to be closed to gays and lesbians even beyond their exclusion of gays from ordination and marriage rites. Many gay people and their friends and families bear the brunt of anti-homosexual ideologies and attitudes. To declare that homosexuality is "incompatible with the Christian faith"and to tell homosexuals that they should either remain celibate or convert to a heterosexual lifestyle is to reject them and even appear to support acts of radicals who use violence against them. This situation has profoundly challenged the faith of many parents and friends of gays and lesbians, and caused them to also feel rejected by their churches.[2.]

This is an account of one family's struggle with the apparent incompatibility of religion and homosexuality.*** They have spent a lifetime of service to their church and their God. This story describes their ups and downs. It documents the events and information which affected them as well as describing their reactions to homophobia. This chronicles their journey through ever widening circles of influence and support—from nuclear family to extended family, from sacred to secular institutions, from local congregation to regional and national church. The authors present a series of challenges and responses regarding the acceptance of gay persons. Their prayer is that the church would truly open its heart, its mind, and its doors to a large and hurting modern day minority group known as GLBTX persons.

FORMAT OF THE BOOK

Each chapter treats a different level of the authors' experience, starting with their nuclear family and going through other levels to considerations of society wide social policy. After a brief **narrative** for each chapter, the authors present documents of two kinds. One type of document is **source material about events** which helped to shape their consciousness. Another type of document is **material by the authors** themselves written to share with their friends, colleagues, and others. Taken all together, the book presents a series of contexts for the authors' personal experiences of and reactions to homophobia.

* Footnotes begin on page 195.

** GLBTX is the generic term currently applied to persons who have a gay. Lesbian, bisexual, transsexual, or indeterminate sexual orientation.

***The names of persons who are noted have been changed for their protection.

Part I. THE CHALLENGE
COMING OUT OF THE CLOSET

Overcoming Barriers to a Positive Self Concept

"Behold, I stand at the door and knock"
(Rev. 3:20 RSV)

by Barbara

THE NARRATIVE

As parents raising three children, we were busy trying to instill the values which we hoped would enable our family to make a Christian witness and a contribution to social justice in the world. Our family was close, and, though we had the typical challenges of raising teenagers, we felt that we were doing a decent job. As challenging as those teen years were, we had little inkling of the trials which we were yet to face.

Our eldest daughter Liz, was a popular and talented student in high school. She was active in band and orchestra, involved in church activities at the local and state levels, and was twice a finalist in the county-wide beauty pageant. She began dating Jim, whom she had met at the United Methodist Youth Congress the summer between her junior and senior year in high school (1980). In college, she continued to be involved in the church, was active in campus politics, and continued to date Jim, who attended the same college. Jim was the president of his fraternity, and Liz was designated the official "sweetheart" of the group.

After graduation, they were married in a beautiful ceremony conducted in the college chapel, on December 14, 1985. Officiating, were the college chaplain; Liz's college advisor; Lloyd Brown, the minister who had married Reg and me; and Reg, my husband, all four of whom were United Methodist clergymen! It was a beautiful ceremony, held in the largest sanctuary in the state of West Virginia.

The newlyweds moved out of state the following summer, where Jim enrolled in graduate school, and Liz took a job as secretary in a local church.

One day in June of 1988, we received a phone call from our daughter. She seemed to be emotionally distraught. Liz said she wanted to speak to one of us in person about a problem, if we could come and see her. As I was attending a professional meeting, Reg drove to see if he could help with this unknown crisis. He would soon learn that it was a crisis faced by many parents, by extended families, the church, and society in general.

After the usual hugs and greetings, Liz and her dad took a walk, during which she explained the source of her trauma to him. In short, after her marriage was consummated, she became concerned that their sexual relationships were not pleasing her. After some time she entered into a therapeutic relationship with a counselor, and finally concluded that she was gay! This announcement left Reg visibly shaken, and, after he sat down on a park bench, he asked what this meant. She said that she and her husband had both been in counseling, and, after considering various alternatives, including staying together, had decided to get divorced. Jim would go on with his life, and she would continue to build a relationship with another young woman whom she had met through the church. Liz and Jim were to remain good friends. That weekend Reg also spent some time with her husband, who was obviously upset, but seemed to be totally involved in their decision. With his admirable maturity and typical humor Jim said that he was handling the situation pretty well. Liz's announcement had caught him off guard but, he said, it was not as surprising to him as it would have been if she had announced that she was becoming a *Republican*!

After spending a couple of days with our daughter and son-in-law, Reg returned home, where he and I would try to work out our feelings about this whole situation. Yes, we were socially progressive and involved in various movements for social justice. We had supported the Civil Rights Movement, and Reg had journeyed to Washington D.C. where he personally heard Dr. Martin Luther King Jr. deliver his famous "I have a Dream" speech. We had opposed the injustices of the war in Vietnam, causing some of our parishioners to wonder about our loyalties, until the Methodist District Superintendent informed the church that Reg and I stood where our Bishop himself stood on this issue. We had come to our political conclusions because of our Christian convictions! We had studied and respected King's way of nonviolence, and tried to learn its principles. We supported women's rights, although neither of us could have been considered a "feminist," but we were standing on shaky ground on the subject of homosexuality.

We had heard the religious arguments against homosexuality, and yet we felt that perhaps it was also a matter of social justice. (Reg had been an advisor to Jim's fraternity, which, he learned, had many gay members. But we had felt that homosexuality was *their problem*, and that we could accept *them* even if we did not understand them.) After Reg and I had gone to counseling, done extensive reading on the subject, and had many conversations with our daughter and her "partner," we gradually began to understand some of the issues surrounding homosexuality. We can't say that this period was easy for us. We were constantly fearful of what abuse might befall our daughter, from job-related discrimination to, perish the thought, the possibility of outright "gay bashing." We all suffered physical ailments relating to the stress of this period. Liz had acute gastro-intestinal problems. During the later, even more stressful period, I suffered from stress-related cardiac problems, and Reg experienced panic attacks. The physical suffering was difficult, but not anything compared to the psychological and spiritual stresses which were still ahead.

Although we were still confused about the "hows" and "whys" of the situation, one thing was certain. We loved our daughter! She was still the same person, and still deserved our support and blessings. "If only the rest of the world could take this view!" we thought. We were to learn that the struggle to "come out of the closet" was not yet finished.

Our other children began to cope with this new revelation about their sister. I am sure that the situation caused them to re-examine their own sexuality. It also challenged them to consider what appropriate responses they might make to their friends who occasionally told anti-homosexual jokes, and revealed certain homophobic feelings. The children gradually learned how to respond to these challenges, and became a great support to their sister, who was still *their* sister.

Our immediate family had learned how to cope with this new revelation. Now we wondered how the extended family would cope.

THE DOCUMENT

Liz's Letter to her Grandparents

Liz was the first grandchild in the family. She had a special bond to her grandparents, but that bond became somewhat weaker after she married and moved away. Here she shares an update on her status.

by Liz, 1988.

Dear Grandma and Grandpa,

Hi! I hope all is well with you both (especially your health). It was nice to see the collection of photos that Grandma took—Mom showed them to me at Thanksgiving. The little ones are sure growing fast!

I'm doing fine. I'm working as a Production Manager for a publishing company in Chicago. It's fun and challenging, but it has confirmed my desire to go to graduate school. The business world can be exciting and I see why many enjoy it, but I can't see myself working in that environment for very long. In the meantime though, it pays the bills and it is a good job!

I wanted to let you know why you haven't heard from me for a while. After a lot of work, discussion, and counseling, Jim and I have decided to separate. We still have a close relationship—just different—and talk with each other often. He is in Jonesburg, Pennsylvania, now and is doing well. This is not as sudden as it may seem. We spent a lot of time working through things before we shared this with anyone. We are both comfortable with our decision and only regret the unease our families may experience. We are also both thankful for the families we have, and their support. ... Love, Liz

Part II COMING OUT FROM PATRIARCHY

Overcoming the Barriers of Male "Superiority" and Familial Loyalty

"Fling wide the portals of your heart"

From the hymn *Lift up your Heads Ye Mighty Gates* by Weiszel, 1635, translated by Catherine Winkworth 1855.

by Barbara

THE NARRATIVE

Liz's struggles to clarify her own identity and our quest as a family to understand her situation were difficult. Yet these conflicts were only to serve as a prelude to another collision which would be even more taxing, a painful clash with our extended family.

Celebrations of the holidays and annual extended family reunions have always been important to us. Our Liz was the first grandchild, and she regularly spent a week each summer with her grandparents in addition to attending the other family events, as did her younger brother and sister. When Liz and Jim were divorced, we did not tell the family that it was based on the issue of her homosexuality. We merely said there was "sexual incompatibility." The family missed Jim's presence at family events, as he was a very congenial, and well-liked person. After a while, Liz began to bring her partner, Rachel, to some family gatherings. The family seemed to accept her as "Liz's friend," and raised no questions about their relationship. We did not know if Mom and Dad recognized this to be a case of the girls' having a "different" sexual orientation. On one occasion Dad said to our son, Cary, "Don't you think that

Rachel seems to be somewhat masculine?" To which Cary replied, "I think she is kind of cute." The conversation roared to a stop with that response, just as Cary had planned. Later, we learned that Dad had telephoned his son-in-law, Sam, a physician in Portland, Oregon, to determine if homosexuality was a physical or mental problem. The response he got was that it was not a physical deficiency, neither was it a mental health problem, as the American Psychiatric Association had taken it off their list of mental illnesses. That seemed to satisfy my father, at least for a while.

Later, during the 1991 Christmas holiday at his home, as most of the extended family were present, including my six brothers and sisters and their families, my father, Russell III, secretly wrote a letter to Liz, who had not been able to attend the event. In the letter he explained that she was, from henceforth, BANNED from her grandparent's home, and would only be welcomed back if and when she changed her sexual orientation! With some input from my brother Randy, my father wrote that Liz had committed an offense "against her father, her grandfather and God." Our younger daughter, Tricia, inadvertently saw the letter open on the table, and informed Reg about it. They were both shocked, but determined not to tell me about it, in hopes that reason would prevail and Dad would change his mind. For six months this secret was kept from me, in hope that I would escape being hurt. Then, in June of 1992, the secret came out.

The entire extended family had been preparing for the family reunion to be held during the summer of 1992. It was to be a very special occasion this year, the celebration of Liz's grandparents' fiftieth anniversary. Everyone was eager to be present at this affair, and express our family solidarity. A week before the Shram reunion, our children surprised us with our own thirtieth anniversary party. Then conversation came around to the approaching fiftieth anniversary celebration of the grandparents. Liz announced that she and Rachel would probably not be going. When I asked why? Liz reluctantly told me that she thought she was not welcome at the celebration. I insisted that Liz must have misunderstood her grandparents (after all, the invitation listed all of our names and said that the party was being hosted by "all the children and grandchildren"). I urged Liz to telephone her grandparents and get clarification. After much hesitation, Liz did call, and, after traditional pleasantries, asked her grandmother if she could come to the anniversary celebration. Grandmother Ramah said she would ask my Dad, and Russell III could be heard in the background saying, "hell no ...". The conversation quickly ended, with Liz sobbing, me in a quandary, and Reg, Cary and Tricia wondering what to do next. I was then told about the letter and the banning. I was devastated, and angry with my family for not telling me earlier.

Needless to say, this had opened Pandora's box to a plethora of emotion-laden discussions and terrible feelings of guilt and rejection for all in the Olson household. It did not take long, however, for me to conclude, "If they will not let Liz come to the anniversary, I will not go either. I must be in solidarity with my daughter, even if they cannot be supportive of us. Do whatever you want," I said to Reg and my children, "but I will not go." This was a terribly difficult situation, for I am the eldest of my siblings, and I was seen as my mother's "right arm" at family gatherings, their preparations, organization and delivery. In a sense, I was forced to choose between my mother and my daughter. I chose my daughter, as did Liz's siblings, and father.

We hoped that my parents would change their mind and lift the ban. (On the other hand, *they* probably were hoping that *we,* but not Liz, would change our mind and come to the family event.) We all hoped that Liz's grandparents would reconsider. Our suitcases were packed, and we were ready to go if and when the reconciling phone call was received. The call never came. We did not go to the anniversary or reunion that year.

It took a long time to be able to communicate further with my parents about this situation, but, once we were more composed, we began a series of correspondence aimed at salvaging the situation. A conflict of wills unfolded and stretched out over a period of three years. It was also difficult to deal with my siblings, as they seemed to follow my father's lead.

Our fervent prayer was that the family would open its heart to Liz.

Sometime letters can catch the tone of a struggle. Here is a letter written by Reg in an attempt to bring some rational and loving conclusion to the situation in 1992.

June 19, 1992

Dear Russ and Ramah:

A lot of pain has recently been shared over some issues which have touched our lives. Your letter to Liz (which she has read to us over the telephone) seems to have marked your concern about a life style that you judged to be inferior and threatening. It was a unilateral act, not prefaced by communication with the parties directly concerned (Liz or us). Perhaps you avoided conversation with us in order to save face. Thank you for your concerns, but they did not help the situation! There was no asking us, "Why did this occur?" or, "can I help?"

The letter represents a rejection of Liz and attempts to change her life style as a condition of acceptance. We attempt to love our family and accept them unconditionally (as God does). Indeed children, parents and grandparents are called to show unconditional love. An analogy to this letter would be if I were to have said that I didn't want

Russ coming to our home as long as he had negative attitudes toward Jews and Blacks. I have not done this because you are family and we love you regardless of your racial and ethnic views.

Are there others who are gay and yet are accepted by you and have been guests in your home? Are there other 'deviant' life styles among family and friends which you have overlooked? This letter was so hurtful that we have tried to comfort and protect those who have been most hurt by it. We didn't want Liz to have to read it. Rachel read only parts to her. I have kept it from Barbara for months in hopes that Russ would soften his attitudes and be more loving. Our not coming to the reunion and anniversary has been very painful to us, especially to Barbara. But, the pain of going and pretending that your rejection of our daughter makes no difference would be even greater.

Liz's situation is a very private matter. Families usually do not discuss their intimate lives with relatives. You can't imagine the pain which Liz has suffered as she has come to grips with her identity! Over the past years great discomfort and soul-searching has lead her to extensive counseling with ministers, psychologists and friends. Amazingly there have been and continue to be good conversations with Jim Normandy. He continues to be one of Liz's best friends and has maintained his support and continual friendship. Liz has experienced great pain and suffering, and we do not want to add to that. It seems to us that her identity has not been a matter of choice, but of necessity.

Those who are close to Liz have likewise experienced pain and suffering, but we have also experienced the love and support of others (both old friends and new) who know something about and/or have experienced this very complex issue. If you are hurt and upset by this situation we are sorry for your pain. But experiencing pain in not sufficient reason to inflict it upon others.

Homosexuality is a difficult issue to understand, and a divisive one. It is hard for us to understand. We all need to be better informed about it. We need to listen to the points of view of those who reject homosexuals and those who accept them. The churches are divided over it, with learned men and women recognizing that Christians in good conscience can differ on this issue.

An act of "tough love," such as your letter represents, assumes that homosexuals are evil, but many say that what is evil is society's homophobic reaction to and treatment of homosexuals. What the scientific community has recognized is that homosexuals are generally normal in every other way of their life, other than their sexual orientation and the modifications of life forced upon them by the disapproving people around them. This situation has not been easy for Liz to adjust to, for the Olson family, or for anyone else. I only hope that you will grow in understanding of this complex issue. To this end I enclose some literature from the United Methodist Church (itself divided over the issue) which I have found helpful as it gives a full range of perspectives.

It is true that one tenth of the population has homosexual 'leanings.' Perhaps it would be good for all of us to learn about the situation in order to help those people make a better adjustment to their situation rather than making them feel unwanted, abnormal and rejected. We wouldn't wish this identity on any others in the family, but we do wish that if anyone else discovered this was their identity they would still feel that they were loved and part of the family.

How shall we treat others who are "different"? Shall we draw a protective circle around ourselves and *shut them out?* Or shall we draw a larger circle and *welcome them* as children of God? This letter is symbolic of our drawing a larger circle, of unconditional love to you and to yours.

May God bless and comfort you. May God bless and continue to guide Liz. May God protect and strengthen us all.

Love, Reg

Reg did not know it then, but this was the start of a series of letters to be written on the same subject over a period of three years. [See Appendix 1 for a chronology of events underlying this correspondence].

THE CORRESPONDENCE

1. Excerpts from the correspondence

We reviewed the events which had taken place

July 29, 1992

Dear Mother and Dad,

... apparently the "letter" was being composed at Christmas when our family arranged our holiday to be with you and Liz, in deference to you, remained in Indiana. While the house is full of family sharing "the Christmas Spirit," daddy is determined to carry out his right to his opinion and send this love/hate letter to his oldest grandchild. Why, at Christmas? Why not ask us about the situation? Is Dad's opinion so sacred that it is more important than the celebration of Christmas, or celebration of family? ...

What you don't seem to understand is that our family wanted to be together for your anniversary. Leaving one [member] behind for any reason was not considered. All five of us had arranged our different schedules for months to be in Brownsburg for your weekend. ... Your Olson grandchildren are very close to you. They have been around longer than most of the others and have spent time with you the others have not chosen to spend. Because of that relationship you have a power with them to both affirm and destroy that doesn't exist with the others. That relationship carried a special responsibility and we grieve its loss, ...

I love you both very much, Barbara

December 1992

Dear Family,

In December, 1992 we sent our annual Christmas letter to family and friends. But this time we sent a Postscript to selected persons who had some knowledge of our absence from the family functions. After describing the events of the preceding year we wrote, "Our nonattendance at the family festivities was not because we were too busy or because we were not interested, or because of sour grapes over the Shrams' not coming to our anniversary (as some have conjectured). In fact our bags were packed throughout the weekend. It was very difficult for us to stay away, and remains a very difficult situation."

We respect you and your feelings, and hope we have not offended you with this letter. We so much wanted to honor the Shrams, see our immediate family members, and visit countless members of the extended family, and friends in June. We regret that the week turned out the way it did. May God grant us all wisdom to deal with such challenges. ...

Sincerely, Reg and Barbara

July 25, 1993

Dear Family,

... It is with a sense of resignation and numbness that I write to say we will not be coming to Brownsburg. All our children are important as human beings and individuals as are all of you. We ask only that the value of a person be placed higher than the value of an issue. ...

Barbara

We wrote that all have a right to their opinions, but that hateful actions, such as a banning, were not acceptable

July 29, 1992 4 AM

Dear Mother and Dad,

... No one denies Dad's right to any and all of his opinions—it is how he acts out these opinions that is degrading, debilitating, and hurtful, especially to him. If a Black, Jewish or homosexual family moved in next door and he proceeded to go expound on his opinions verbally or in writing he could be arrested!

I love you both very much, Barbara

August 11, 1992

Dear Family,

... We are not being inflexible or unreasonable about anyone's attitudes or opinions. I think we are able to allow others to have their own opinions, just as we hope that others will respect our right to have ours. ... The bottom line, it seems to us, is that our daughter Liz is banned from her grandparents' home. This is not an issue of attitudes or opinions, but a question of actions. We cannot accept this or condone it. ... Love, Reg

October 8, 1992

Dear Family,

... In a large family we all learn to tolerate idiosyncrasies. Disagreements over attitudes are O.K., they reflect the differences of the larger society. Differences are all right. But the bottom line came when our daughter Liz was told that she was not welcome in the Shram household unless she became a different person. The rejection of Liz's personhood was like drawing a line in the sand. ... Love, Reg Olson

July 25, 1993

Dear Family,

... The Shram household has, in the past been a forgiving family. I have always felt accepted even though my politics were different from theirs. As the Arby's commercial says, "Different is good." I have accepted you all despite differences in opinion. You are family, not chosen because of a need to influence values or attitudes, but chosen because of a deep and abiding love for Barbara, a love which has grown over the years. When we visit the Shram clan we do not view others as representatives of categories— "married," "divorced," "unmarried," etc. We view you as family. ...

With love and respect, Reg Olson

We asked questions about communication. We noted that my parents had never consulted us about the "facts" of

our daughter's situation; that they had expected us to consult with them and ask for help in the situation; and we realized that continuing dialogue was needed. Mom wrote the following:

July 6, 1992

Dear Barb and Reg,

... Reg, I appreciate your letter and have read it several times but my mind just isn't working well enough to write an answer. It has given me some sleepless nights but just give me time. ... We love you both so much you know and we are willing to work on our problem. Your dad is not well and we can not expect him to react to A SITUATION AS A THIRTY YEAR OLD. He reacts to everything differently but with tender loving care we get along pretty fine. We have fifty years of love to build on and try to make things work for us. But I can't expect him to discard his strong beliefs. I have to admit my personal experiences follow his beliefs too. Well enough of this heavy stuff. Just remember we love you all. Let's keep lines of communication open.

Mom

July 29, 1992

Dear Mother and Dad,

... Communication requires a message, a sender, a receiver, and decoding. You say the message sent was one of love. The receiver (and our whole family) decoded it as one of hate. The results have been hateful, not loving, hurtful, not healing, and are probably irreconcilable.

Why attack Liz? Why not ask us or her if you really were concerned? We would have been willing to discuss with you what has been a difficult learning experience spanning the past four years—if you wanted to listen and discuss and not argue the rights of heterosexuality alone. ...

I love you both very much, Barbara

Christmas, 1992

Dear Russ and Ramah,

... We have shared feelings and ideas in phone calls and letters back and forth. We are glad for the channels of communication. Has any progress been made in healing the rupture? What is progress? Does it mean the changing of Liz's sexual orientation? Does it mean family acceptance of Liz as a person? I think we need to test ourselves and see if we have been hearing one another's concerns. Here is our good faith understanding of what I think we have heard, as the concerns that you have experienced and expressed. Please read them as an attempt to seriously hear and understand where you are. Please write and correct any misinterpretations so that we can communicate more effectively. I also ask that you attempt the same exercise of telling us in good faith, what you have heard us saying and writing . ...

Sincerely, Reg Olson

May 18, 1993

Dear Randy,

... While mother and I are communicating at certain levels, we are doing so at their request to not discuss homosexuality or Liz's situation. Finding something to talk about is difficult when you consider this and the extreme hurt I still feel about last year's anniversary events. ...

Love, Your Sister Barbara

Sometimes letters disguise discomfort. At other times they were expressions of the depth of pain we had experienced.

July 29, 1992, 4 A.M

Dear Mother and Dad,

As you can tell, I'm not sleeping and my eyes are filled with tears. I thought I was getting to a point that communication might be possible—I'm not sure. The pain has been so intense that it has been impossible for me to communicate. ...

Where do we go from here? I do not know. The experience I have had is much like the death of both parents, only worse, because one can heal from that experience and take comfort in beautiful memories. These memories were shattered in their making and will always be like a knife turning in my heart. ...

I love you both very much, Barbara

August 11, 1992

Dear Family,

... Liz did not initiate a confrontation in June over whether or not she could go to Brownsburg. Because Barbara did not know about the letter from the Shrams she urged Liz to call (when I was out of the house) and see if she was welcome. (Liz had said that she was getting mixed signals about whether or not she should come.) She was told Sunday that she was not to come. Liz did not ask us to go to Brownsburg, nor has she in any way suggested what our actions should be... . The hurt and pain was not created by any actions of our family, it occurred as a result of a letter which banned a granddaughter... (this was an attempt to move from blame to an expression of hurt.)

Love, Reg

March 18, 1994

Dear Randy,

... There have been times when I wanted to forget my extended family. In fact this has been necessary to save my mental health. All of us have expressed from time to time that we just can't handle more for the time being because our emotions are so intense. ...

Love to all of you, Barbara

My Dad wrote the following expression of pain

January 16, 1993

REG,

We have not changed. We still love the same GOD we always have, we still have the same Nature we always have, we still have the same high ideals we always have, we love our children and grandchildren as we always have including Liz *of ten years ago [emphasis added].*

You and Liz and Barbara are the ones who have changed. We have but one question to ask of Liz, not You or Barbara, but of Liz. ... The question is (WHY)???

Love, Ramah and Russ Shram

We recognized that both Church and Society were split on the issue of the acceptance of homosexuality

October 8, 1992

Dear Family,

... National church bodies are struggling with this issue (they are divided over it). We are fully aware that many church people oppose homosexuality.

Are you fully aware that many urge the churches to be more open to those who are gay? ...

Love, Reg Olson

Christmas,1992

Dear Russ and Ramah,

... Society in general is polarized over the issue of homosexuality, with many persons in society (and the churches condemning the gay lifestyle. ...

Sincerely, Reg Olson

Attempts to Educate the Family About Homosexuality: Reg tried some conflict resolution techniques and asked questions about communication

Christmas, 1992

Dear Russ & Ramah,

... It seems that you have said the following:

1. You are upset with Liz's being a lesbian, for you see this as "unnatural," and "un-Christian."

2. You think you should have been consulted when we learned about this situation, because you think you might have been able to prevent Liz's becoming a lesbian.

3. You have wanted to help Liz change because you love her and want "what is right for her."

4. In order to motivate her to change, you used what some people call "tough love," and said she is not accepted in your household unless she changes.

5. You have experienced resentment over what you perceive as Liz's "coming between" Barbara and her parents.

6. You fear that Liz is a bad example for her nieces and nephews, and also fear that she will "hit on" one of them, doing physical harm, or turning them into gay persons.

Is this the crux of what you have said? Have I heard your thoughts and your feelings? Please let me know where I am incorrect about what you have said.

It seems to me that there is some common ground. Please correct me if I am wrong, but I think we can agree on the following:

1. The challenge of accepting Liz's new identity has been traumatic for her, the Olsons, and the Shrams.

2. Both the Olsons and the Shrams want the best for their children and grandchildren and would like to help them steer away from harmful things.

3. We fear for Liz's safety and well-being, even as we also fear for the safety and well-being of all young women (and men).

4. We believe the bonds between parents and children, especially mothers and daughters, are very important.

5. We want Liz's future to be bright, for her to fulfill her God-given talents and accomplish good things for herself and the world.

6. Liz is an adult, with her own needs and abilities. She has a life of her own to live.

7. When society rejects a person's lifestyle the person may respond by rejecting the society, "dropping out," trying to become acceptable to the society, or trying to change the society.

8. The Bible says much which could be interpreted as a rejection of homosexuality.

Do we agree on any of these things. Would you share any of these ideas but prefer to word them differently? ...

Love, Reg

Reg raised the issue of whether people choose to become homosexual

October 8, 1992

Dear Family,

... Long ago the American Psychiatric Association said that homosexuality is not a disease, or an aberration. But, we may ask, Who would *choose* to be an object of scorn and follow this life style? That is the point. More and more people are beginning to tell us that, for the most part, people do not *choose* to be homosexuals. They just own up to being what they already are. A high church official recently told us just that. Did we *choose* to be heterosexuals? I'll bet we didn't, it just seemed natural. But for homosexuals *their* sexuality seems "natural". ...

Love, Reg Olson

What about the possibility that other members of the family might come out as homosexuals?

July 29, 1992

Dear Mother and Dad,

... If one of my nieces or nephews had been similarly banned, I would not have been in Brownsburg either.. Both Reg and I hope that if our nieces and nephews face difficult challenges they know that we will listen and are concerned. ...

I love you both very much, Barbara

October 8, 1992

Dear Family,

... How would you feel if your child was told that they were not allowed to go to someone else's home? Not welcome? Excluded? Written off? What if Irma, Cary, Eliza , Ann , Carol, or Mary were excluded from a gathering which was advertised as an event to which the "children and grandchildren" invited the world? How kindly would you feel? Would you go anyway and say, "It's okay for you to reject my child?"

Love, Reg Olson

May 18, 1993

Dear Randy,

... None of you will understand until you face a socially unacceptable situation with a child or loved one. Then, I hope and pray that God speaks to those involved in a way of love and reconciliation. And that rejection and banning and forcing of opinions are found to be the hurtful, dogmatic and arrogant actions which they are. ...

Love, Your Sister Barbara

Reg noted that we support our children

July 29, 1992

Dear Mother and Dad,

... Reg and I are both proud of all three of our kids. They are responsible, considerate, loving adults. None of them have or would inflict hurt directly on you. However, if you *choose* to be hurt by decisions they make to have better, worthwhile, charitable lives, then that is your decision. ...

I love you both very much, Barbara

October 8, 1992

Dear Family,

... Why didn't we go? Because our children count to us. We learned family values of loyalty and support, and when the crunch came we had to practice those values. We were denied the opportunity to share in the anniversary weekend because of an intolerant act. ..."

Love, Reg Olson

I also asked if my parents had any friends who were secretly gay

July 29, 1992

Dear Mother and Dad,

... Apparently there are different criteria for your acceptance of friends and family. Was your anniversary and reunion list checked thoroughly for approvable lifestyles? I submit that there were many lifestyles represented. What about sexual practice? Do you know everything that occurs behind closed doors of all your children, grandchildren and friends? Of course not. Nor do we about you or each other. This is a private part of relationships and normally it is respected. ...

I love you both very much, Barbara

Reg insisted that sexual practices are a private matter

June 19, 1992

Dear Russ and Ramah,

... Liz's situation is a very private matter. Families usually do not discuss their intimate lives with relatives. You can't imagine the pain which Liz has suffered as she has come to grips with her identity! Over the past years great discomfort and soul-searching has lead her to extensive counseling with ministers, psychologists and friends. ...

Love, Reg

August 11, 1992

Dear Family,

... Liz and we have been faulted for not seeking counsel from our extended family as Liz sought to understand her identity. We chose to keep a very private matter confidential and not force a difficult issue on others. Apparently, all the family has talked about Liz for some time without ever asking her or us for our perspective. In other words, Liz's banning was based on hearsay. ...

Love, Reg

I regretted that my siblings had not shown support to us

July 29, 1992

Dear Mother and Dad,

... I spent the whole week praying, hoping that the situation would change and we would be welcomed as a family. I yearned for the phone to ring and someone to ask "What is going on?" No one did! I find out later that all my brothers and sisters knew about the letter and yet were not concerned about its affect on their niece or our family. ...

... In our complete bewilderment and pain we discussed with Sam and Sheba what possible alternatives remain. I asked them what they would do if one of their girls received a letter similar to Liz's for any reason. Sam responded, "I wouldn't be going to Brownsburg. ..."

I love you both very much, Barbara

Some family support did eventually emerge, from some family members

December 27, 1993

Dear Barb, Reg, and Family,

... It is such a pleasure to be part of your family and it saddens me terribly to think of a all the time you are letting go by not getting together. You are missed very much and especially by your mother. I hope and pray there can be some sort of reconciliation in the new year. I want you to know you and your family are welcome to visit me anytime you please.

Love, Cousin Jenna

On the occasion of my birthday my aunt Phyllis wrote:

April 5, 1993

Dear Barb,

... I admire your attitude about a situation which I'm sure is most difficult. I certainly understand that your first loyalty is to your immediate family. It has got to be tough not having the support of your parents (& siblings?) Liz certainly must have had some terrific struggles within before she reached this stage in life.

I can only say that you *all* have my empathy and concern.

Love, Aunt Phyllis

My brother had been admonished by his wife to make amends for his part in the banning

February 21, 1994

Dear Barbara,

... I sincerely hope that someday you will forgive us and accept us as the failures of your expectations that we are, and come home to Brownsburg to show your love for us as we would like you to. I have come a long way since that fateful day in late December 1991. I have come to hate that event, as Priscilla continues to point out how wrong I was to have voiced an opinion, let alone support Dad's. ...

Love Always, Randy

I responded to him saying,

March 18, 1994

Dear Randy,

... As I write this I realize that I do not want it to sound negative. While there has been much pain and hurt, we could all be reaching a time for new growth and deeper more meaningful and caring relationships with one another. ...

Love to all of you, Barbara

Reg shared his appreciation for the support of friends

October 8, 1992

Dear Family,

... Yes, it has been hard to accept the situation. We have had countless conversations with ministers, counselors, and friends, virtually all of whom have said that it [homosexuality] is not a sin, that Liz is a good person, and that she is indeed loved by God. Shouldn't she be accepted as a person too, even if her orientation differs from our own?. ...

Love, Reg Olson

July 25, 1993

Dear Family,

... We thank God that in these difficult times we have been comforted by countless friends— the Jones, Brown and Lisa, the Smyths, the Klemers and others. I guess that even though they are not blood relatives, they understand the meaning of family, and have shown us all, even Liz, love and acceptance. ...

With love and respect, Reg Olson

We asked what was to be done, acceptance or rejection

July 29, 1992

Dear Mother and Dad,

... Where do we go? We are staying right here. Our circle is wide enough for you if you want to be a part. ...

I love you both very much, Barbara

Despite the raw feelings we experienced, we continued to express love for my parents

August 11, 1992

Dear Family,

...We have stated clearly that others are welcome in our home. When it is clear that we and

Liz are welcome elsewhere we will feel comfortable going. We are not giving an ultimatum. Just as the doors were closed, they can be opened.

Love Reg

July 25, 1993

Dear Family,

... Our door is open and our welcome mat is out to all of you.

Barbara

March 18, 1994

Dear Randy,

We are keeping all of you in our thoughts and prayers. ... We wish you all the best.

Love to all of you, Barbara

Thinking that this issue might never be resolved, I made one last attempt. I continued with a challenge that my mother come out of the closet as the grandparent of a gay child!

January 27, 1995

Dear Mother Shram,

This morning I find that I am particularly distressed with your saying that you love us very much and after *three* years you feel it is OK to ban your granddaughter from your home. So I am going to be as direct as I feel. Love doesn't create situations like this estrangement! Love gives us a willingness to learn, to accept what we don't understand, to reach out and build bridges, not lock doors. You are a different person than Dad. I acknowledge that change in him is unlikely now. I just wish someone would have said NO to him three years ago.

You are capable of learning and gathering new information. The Board of CMC is made up of a number of people your age and older. They are open to new information and have been very supportive of us and warm to Liz and Rachel when they've been here.

Your granddaughter did not choose to be Lesbian. She chose to give Jim the opportunity for a full relationship when she realized that God had not created her as a heterosexual being. If you want to place blame, her genes came from us. So blame me, Reg, you, Dad, but for heavens sake she should not be thrown away for being what she was created to be.

The actions Dad and You Chose to take have caused our family great pain. These actions have been adopted by all of my brothers and sisters because of their ignorance, inexperience, and love for you.

We have tried to meet all of you part way by coming to Brownsburg and attending last year's family reunion. This was taken as our admission that Liz is wrong and not that we were trying to bridge a gap. No reaching out has occurred in terms of any of my siblings or my parents. Yes, you have written to Liz and that is appreciated. But, how would you feel to receive letters from someone who banned you from their home, which are written as though nothing is amiss, and include stories of activities you are not welcome to participate in and about people, cousins in fact, that you've never seen and are not welcome to see. That Hurts!

I haven't heard from Mary in a year and a half, except for a few minutes at Roy's last summer. How do you think that makes me feel? We didn't ban them, they've chosen to ignore us.

We've waited for three years for something to change. I don't want you telling people that we are too busy to visit. Tell them that you banned our daughter from your home and we think that's inappropriate. Tell them she's a lesbian, that she has a good education, that she owns a nice home with her partner Rachel, that she has a good job, that she is highly respected by her professional peers, that she and Rachel are active in a United Church of Christ congregation, and that Liz's parents love her and helped create her as the child of God which she is. Therefore, we are not comfortable being in a place where she and Rachel are banned.

In other words, I want you to talk about it! You will find all kinds of responses, but I am sure you will be surprised by others who have a similar story, who are willing to talk, who care about you and what you are experiencing. This is an opportunity for all of us to grow and God helps when we are willing to listen.

Mother, this situation will not resolve itself by drawing a line in the sand. It requires the same type of determination to rectify it that created it in the first place. Letters which do not in some way express concern about the schism only deny the situation and hurt more.

Cary and Michelle's wedding plans have been deeply affected by all of this. That is wrong. We've had many discussions about how to handle this. They've had to decide not to involve any of Cary's extended family in the wedding itself because they don't want to deal with possible rejection for themselves, or Liz and Rachel. We also expect that most will find an excuse not to come and we are trying to be braced for that. But, I keep praying that God will intervene and open the hearts of a family to a granddaughter and niece who is a human being God created her to be, as we all are. That would be the best possible outcome I can think of in this new year.

We all want to be loved and accepted unconditionally by those we love. Thanks for letting me be direct.

I do love you. Barbara.

Reconciliation

After I received this letter my mother called after getting Dad's consent to lift the ban. He had been in failing health and had Alzheimer's disease. There is some question as to whether or not he was fully aware when Mom said to him, "This whole thing has gone on too long. Can't we invite Liz back into the fold?" Dad apparently said, "yes." This was all my mother needed to welcome Liz (and us) back.

After this, Mother was very welcoming to Liz AND Rachel. Years later, Ramah graciously acted as a surrogate grandmother to Rachel when her two grandmothers died within about a month of each other. Mom said to Rachel, "You know you still have one grandmother."

A Christmas "thank you" from Liz and Rachel

December, 1997

Dear Barb & Reg,

... Liz and I are attempting a new ritual this year: each day of Advent each of us writes a brief note to someone dear to us. Today I/we choose the two of you!

Every day, and perhaps more and more all the time, we are reminded of how blessed we are to have the two of you in our lives. Being a parent, being the parent of a daughter, being the parents of a lesbian daughter, being the parent of a lesbian daughter with a long time partner — none of these come with any guarantee, any guidelines. But, hopefully, they all bring a certain measure of joy and love and give back to you even a portion of what you offer us. We love you both very much.

We enjoyed—each in our own way—sharing the Thanksgiving with you in Brownsburg. We wish we knew how to be in many places all at once at Christmas. We look forward to being with you to ring in the new year. ... Though we will only be there in spirit, we hope your Open House is a warm and memorable event (with lots of left-over cookies!)

Have a beautiful Christmas!

Much love, Rachel and Liz.

2. Interpretation— Family Solidarity or Patriarchal Privilege?

by Barbara

As we look back at these events the reasons for the family's rejection are still unclear to us. Was it a case of simple homophobia? Was the issue really just a question of a threat to family solidarity? Or was there another dynamic involved, namely the preservation of patriarchy, or, male privilege?

My mother was a somewhat independent thinker, and a credentialed social worker who worked for the county for a number of years, despite my father's objections. So maybe patriarchy was always *somewhat* in jeopardy in their household. Family events and reunions were almost always held at the Shrams, with a focus on the eldest living male. In addition to my brothers and sisters and their families, the reunions were usually attended by a variety of Dad's cousins and others. My father's cousin had done some extensive family genealogy work, tracing his side of the family back several generations to their German origins. Mom and Dad had traveled to the family home in Germany and met some living members of the family. "The family" almost always meant my father's, *Russell III's* family.

Dad valued and defended male-based traditions. I remember that he had written in his letter that Liz had committed an offense against her father, her grandfather and God (also a masculine figure?). Perhaps my father had resented the appearance of Liz's lack of family loyalty. After her marriage, she and her husband had only attended one family function.

Ironically, however, Liz and Rachel had been involved in many family gatherings. They had visited Brownsburg in 1989 and the Shrams took them out to eat at a nice restaurant. What caused my father to issue his ultimatum December, 1991? Was it because Liz was already seen as a threat to family solidarity? Was it because Liz had given books with inclusive themes as holiday gifts to the other grandchildren? Was it because of growing societal conservative political and religious opposition to homosexuality? Was it because of Randy's apparent complicity, complete with biblical support? Homosexuality IS a threat to patriarchy and male dominance!

The banning could be seen as an attempt to reassert patriarchal domination. Perhaps my father decided to take the initiative from Liz, whom he saw to be rejecting the family (and male dominance), and attempted to control the situation, by making make HIS vehement rejection of her.

But Dad didn't expect a ripple effect, with his

daughter ready to challenge him. We only record the view from the Olson's family. What was going on in the Shram household? Did they talk about homosexuality? (probably not). Did they just submit to patriarchal authority? The second reunion in 1993 was a test of wills. The Olsons did not give in. Various efforts were unleashed to restore patriarchal authority. There was the pretext of allowing Liz to come back, which was exposed by Barbara and Reg, with anger. There were requests from my siblings to visit and reconcile with my MOM. I wonder if my mother was experiencing the wrath of my father and various efforts to control her during this time?

The cracks widened. Priscilla challenged her husband Randy's action in helping his father write the infamous "letter." This resulted in his apology to me. Our friends (some of whom were mutual friends of the Shrams) expressed their support of Liz and her family. Perhaps some of the correspondence began to have an effect. In 1994 the Olsons went to the reunion to try to have an impact and break the deadlock, but we reiterated our support for Liz and our willingness to make the rupture permanent.

There was a decline of patriarchy. My father had experienced a heart attack, cancer, and strokes. Despite these infirmities he continued to try to maintain his authority. However, his judgment and mannerisms did not seem appropriate for a patriarch. His own children began laughing openly at his behaviors. How sad it is when legitimacy is on the wane. My father was being treated as a relic of the past.

Roy, the eldest male in my family, did not assert his patriarchal authority or support for his father's position. Communication continued. Randy was won over. Mom got Dad's (unknowing?) consent to lift the ban. When our son Cary announced his impending wedding there was the perception that the whole sad state of affairs might affect Cary's wedding, and family solidarity might be further shattered, but enough was enough. The family gave broad support for the wedding of Michelle and Cary.

Mom's ultimate openness to Liz and Rachel was not emulated by Liz's uncles. After the reconciliation, and Liz and Rachel's attendance at family gatherings, the men in the family continued to act defensively, shielding their children from any unsupervised contact with Liz and Rachel.

Dad entered a nursing home in 1997. The family held a private communion service at the nursing home, with Reg officiating. The summer reunion, a symbol of patriarchy and family solidarity, was held that weekend, and Dad died during the next week. A memorial service was held the following Sunday, in Church, with Liz and Rachel present, and Reg preaching. "Proper respect" was shown for Russell III. Did patriarchy also die? Have homophobic attitudes changed? Although the women in-laws in the family have shown strength and independence, they have not publicly challenged patriarchy. Family "peace" has been restored, at least for the moment.

We prayed that our whole family would someday open their hearts to our daughter and others like her.

Part III THE CHURCH COMING OUT FROM SODOM

Overcoming the Barrier of Closed Church Doors

"I would rather be a doorkeeper in the house of my God than dwell in the tents of wickedness"
(Psalm 84:10 b,c RSV)

by Reg

This passage could be claimed by both homophobic church people and supporters of GLBTX persons. The crucial question is what constitutes "wickedness?" The former group insists that homosexuals are wicked and their active presence in the church would pollute the Body of Christ. The latter group, to which we adhere, asserts that homophobia is itself a form of wickedness. We want to influence the gate-keepers of the church to open their doors to the vast number of GLBTX persons, their families and friends who have been alienated.

A. THE LOCAL CHURCH

"Flee for your lives, do not look back ..."
(Gen. 19:17b RSV)

THE NARRATIVE

For several years we had received moral support from clergy and lay members of our local church. This support gave us a somewhat false sense of ease as we were thinking that most clergy of our denomination were open to and accepting of homosexuality. This bubble was to be burst somewhat rudely. I was the Director of the Christian

Center, an ecumenical program of seven different Protestant denominations offered to the students and staff of Oxbridge University. When I was first interviewed for the job a member of the search committee asked if I had any experience working with homosexuals. I confirmed some limited experience, but was not yet willing to come out as a parent of a lesbian daughter.

Later I learned about the Reconciling Congregation program. It consisted of local congregations that feel compelled to give support to homosexuals by going on record as being officially "open and affirming," etc. I thought that our Christian Center might investigate this program. After preliminary discussions with some board members about homosexuality, I raised the question in a board meeting. I asked if the board would like to learn about the reconciling movement, examine what this designation entailed, and look into the process of becoming a reconciling campus ministry. We were not to vote on becoming a reconciling ministry, but, rather, to investigate what that status entailed. Then one member of the board, a local pastor, said rather authoritatively, "I don't know about the rest of you, but I think the folks at my church would not support this, and might be rather offended by it." Although I was somewhat surprised by this declaration, I was not ready to make a case which might become divisive, at least for the time being. I learned later that several members of the pastor's congregation, who were also on the board, took him to task for his opposition to our investigation. They felt that the pastor personally did not accept homosexuals either. The church was divided on this issue, both locally and nationally. This split is not to be easily overcome.

As time went by my wife and I became increasingly impatient with the church's failure to support its own children who had come out of the closet. In fact, it became apparent that many people who committed hate crimes against suspected homosexuals felt they had the support of the church, the Bible and God. So we began to write positional papers to prod others to examine the issue of acceptance of homosexuals. It became clear to us that many conservative Christians believed that the Bible was opposed to homosexuality. Many traced this opposition to the story of Sodom and Gomorrah. After researching this story, I gathered my thoughts into a paper for distribution to family, friends and others who were struggling with the issue.

We had several meetings in our home, having invited persons whom we believed were open to the issue of homosexuality, that we might support one another. Some did not know the official position of our denomination on homosexuality, and were surprised to hear about it. Others described their own struggles with homosexuality, involving their children, neighbors, friends, and colleagues. An outgrowth of our home meetings was the ultimate establishment of a chapter of PFLAG, Parents and Friends of Gays and Lesbians, in our local community. This is a support group for those who are going through struggles similar to our daughter's and ours.

As it became clear to more people that we were "gay friendly" we were asked by some members of our congregation to speak in Sunday school class about our personal experience with a gay daughter, and a rejecting family. At first we felt uncomfortable doing this, but then we realized that this was a cathartic testimony to others who might be going through similar struggles. We were always very sure to end with a declaration that the love of God had, indeed, triumphed.

Others in our congregation asked what the church could do to be more open and friendly toward both homosexuals and heterosexuals. They worked on various "official" statements which might declare our openness. People thought that these welcoming statements might be printed in the church bulletin. We noted that the problem was not just how to *tell* outsiders that we were open and accepting people, but that we had to confront the question of whether or not we *were really* an open congregation. Wouldn't it be dishonest for us to welcome homosexuals into our midst, only to have them learn that there were many homophobic church members here?

At a Christian Center Symposium on Race, Gender and Orientation we heard a poignant statement recounted by a gay woman. "I could never feel welcome in your church," she had told the members of the local church's Church and Society meeting on "openness." She said that "politics" is a part of it— if the national church is anti-gay, and if the local congregation is not welcoming she would feel especially uncomfortable. Never-the-less, she said, "I can feel and appreciate the welcome which some individuals share with me."

Another gay person described a meeting he had had with the pastor of a local church. He said, " When I went to him before I joined the church and was wrestling with the problem of whether to become a mentor for a confirmand, the pastor responded by saying, 'We don't ask people if they cheat on their income tax, whether they have committed adultery,' and a few more *sins*. That response has recently come back to haunt me. I have always lived with the 'wrong,' and severely psychologically deleterious notion that my sexual orientation, and especially acting on it by entering a loving partnership and having a sexual relationship, was indeed not only 'wrong' but a sin. [I should have responded to my pastor by saying], 'I don't think I am entering the church as a sinner.'"

This same person left the United Methodist Church and started attending the Mount Auburn Presbyterian Church in Cincinnati. It was not that the Presbyterian Church as a denomination was more open and affirming, but that this local congregation was exceptionally welcoming. An article in the *Cincinnati Enquirer* (January 6, 2001, A-1, A-4) referred to Mount Auburn as a place where, "Church leaders are openly disobedient to the national denomination by ordaining gay and lesbian members as elders." About a third of the members are gay and lesbian, according to the Rev. Steven Van Kuiken, and the church has held same sex ceremonies. Worship services also are diverse. On any given Sunday, the songs range from classical to folk to African music. "We're not real rigid when it comes to doctrine," says the Rev. Mr. Van Kuiken. "People are given a lot of room to search and find their own way." Mount Auburn was named as one of the top 300 Protestant churches in the nation by a study conducted by Paul Wilkes, of the University of North Carolina at Wilmington. [3.]

We continued to hope and pray that our church and its pastor might have an epiphany experience on the issue of openness to homosexuals. Barbara asked that some of our articles be published in the church newsletter. The pastor refused the request. During a visit to our home he indicated his extreme discomfort with the issue, and his desire not to divide the church over this controversy. He said that he felt torn between different elements of the congregation. He even seemed somewhat depressed. Later, Barbara wrote an apology to him for any pressure he felt from her. We could not expect that the whole future of the church's response to the gay community hinged on the pastor's attitudes. Of course a pastor is a key player in the struggle, setting the tone according to his or her priorities, but clergy come and go, and it is the congregation which ultimately lives out the tone of openness. [4.]

While visiting the Church of the Good Shepherd United Church of Christ, a reconciling congregation in Ann Arbor, Michigan, we were very impressed with the length to which church people might go to make strangers, members of minorities, and particularly homosexuals feel welcome.

In an attempt to prompt local churches to grapple with the question of HOW open they were to persons of gay sexual orientations I later developed a questionnaire for use by churches. (This is found in Appendix 2.) The struggle with homophobia was, however, not just a congregational struggle. It was a struggle faced by the national denominations too.

THE DOCUMENTS

Here are some of the events which affected us and some papers we wrote in response.

1. A Reconciling Congregation

We received an e-mail describing one congregation's struggle with being Open.

Anonymous

Hi—Forgot to tell you. On October 8, CUMC/WF will vote on a Statement of Reconciliation which essentially says that everyone is welcome in our congregation. We've been working on this for almost five years. We've had several folks leave just because we talked about it, the latest being Dora and her husband. Harold and Shelly are probably going to leave too.

Now a hate letter has surfaced about another pastor—anyone who is single now is targeted as being gay—and we are mentioned as a 'liberal loving church ... [which] is going to take in gays and lesbians.' The United Methodist Church at Hunter's Creek was torched by an arsonist a couple of weeks ago. The pastor there is a broad-minded guy (not single) and it's being treated as a hate crime. So, the FBI now has a copy of the afore-mentioned letter and we are all a little nervous about what might happen. We have a new bishop, who just arrived September 1, and he probably thought he was coming to nice, tranquil and bland state.

I'll keep you posted.

Hi—Our statement of reconciliation passed this afternoon by a 135-14 vote. We were hoping for a 75% vote and so are overwhelmed by this 90% endorsement. Lots of folks were praying for us: two bishops, congregations in Kansas City, Missouri, and Columbus, OH, the Christian Center at the U. of Missouri, the 55 members of my Academy for Spiritual Formation (11 different denominations from 15 states), a woman from our conference was walking the labyrinth at Grace Church in San Francisco praying for us. I think it really made a difference—folks kept saying that they were at peace no matter how the vote went and that they really felt buoyed and sustained. I am so proud of this congregation. It seems so simple just to say that everyone is welcome here but we live in a time when even that is controversial. Now we'll deal with the fall-out. Dora and her husband have left the church and we think that Harold and Shelly are not far behind. However, we have new folks coming precisely because we were considering the statement.

2. There's An Elephant In Our Sanctuaries!

Barbara wrote a paper for our church newsletter entitled, "There is an elephant in our sanctuaries," which related to our local church, but also to the churches at large.

by Barbara Olson 1999

Society has decided, except in a few locales, that persons of any other sexual orientation than us heterosexuals shall be treated as lesser citizens. Equal rights are generally not extended to homosexuals in terms of workplace security, health care family packages, hate crime protection, adoption rights, and subtle degradation.

The Church is being challenged to respond to this treatment of a group of God's Children. Yes, God's Children! Gays, Lesbians, Bisexuals are all created by God, in his image, just as God created you and me. Instead of heeding God's call to accept ALL of his or her children, most congregations have chosen to reflect society's hateful reaction to a human condition that has been forced to hide in the "closet" for centuries. It is said that Gays are welcome, but they must repent of their homosexual sin. Most churches want to cure this "illness" and have decided that sexual orientation is chosen as a way of life. Have you given thought to how easily you might 'choose' your sexuality? Would you choose to be ill-treated and de-humanized by society if you had that choice? Probably not. Another way to consider sexual orientation is much as we do eye color, hair color, voice pitch, skin color and other human condition variations. Let's place heterosexuality on one end of a continuum, where we might place blonde hair, blue eyes or very pale skin. On the other end of the continuum will be black hair, dark-brown or black eyes, dark skin and homosexuality. In the center of this progression is bisexuality. Due to societal pressures, persons do choose to change their appearance. We have these pressures to thank for anorexia, skin cancer, unhealthy bleached hair etc. We also have these pressures to thank for most persons choosing to act as heterosexuals unless they are in the 10 per cent at the homosexual end of the continuum. This might explain why there are persons who have been "cured" or became homosexual after a heterosexual relationship. They have chosen to try to fit society's mold or they are unable to continue to ignore the humanity God created in them.

Sadly, when many Gays are asked if they are Christian, they respond that it is impossible to be gay and Christian. The treatment of Gays in our churches is so abominable that it is easier to be "out" as a gay person in society than in church. We are called by God to Love our Neighbors, Judge Not, and Live Our Lives as Servants. Nowhere do we hear that homosexuals are not loved by God. Scriptures may reflect some obscure references to same-sex behavior. But it says far more about borrowing money (usury), divorce, adultery, pride, wealth and not responding to God's will. We have managed to reinterpret these human behaviors according to our needs. Why then do we not reinterpret the obscure passages that are readily used to assail our homosexual citizens, in light of the world today. It should be recognized that women are no longer owned by men, racially we are equal, and that both male and female children are equal in God's sight. We have been slow to answer God's prodding on these issues, but we are finally answering the call to treat all God's children with compassion, unless they are homosexual.

God's word is a matter of ongoing revelation, not a stagnant document written nearly 2000 years ago. The Bible is a handbook, a guide, a manuscript to study and evaluate, a history to help us know our God and Christ in a specific period and place. The Bible should not be a club to use in an act of intolerance, should not be interpreted within arbitrary constraints of our limited knowledge, is not an English document nor the King James Version its original writing. Ironically, various interpretations of the Bible have been our attempt to give the masses access to the 'word' and to attempt understanding within the context of the time of the interpretation. Why are we no longer open to this call by God that the plan is constantly being revealed to us? Is our relationship to God not one of growth through prayer or communication?

The Elephant in our sanctuary is a huge issue that we are ignoring, studying within our own biases, or Biblical righteousness without accepting God's present word. This Elephant will be present in our Conferences this summer, but most of us have chosen to step away from the conversation. Unfortunately, those who use the Bible as a club, or have chosen to act superior to their fellow human beings are carrying the charge. Is this God's will? Women and Blacks waited for hundreds of years to be treated as equals, but the persons mentioned above are still fretting about doing this and occasionally, they commit hate crimes in the name of God. Do we want to grow in favor with God and people or just persons over whom we can wield power?

It is your choice, for God has given us the right to choose our behavior and action toward others. It is time that the church takes God's call to love ALL persons, seriously. God does not condone our continued ignorance of diversity created in us all. The Elephant is asking for our attention. The issue of Gays and Lesbians in our Churches stands to divide us as other issues have before. Can we truly open our hearts and ears to God's word and will, making All God's children truly a part of Christ's Church?

3. RUMS Profiles—Stories of Victims of Homophobia

Being concerned about the way the church had alienated many talented persons, some of whom had been candidates for ministry, I wrote and distributed this paper to friends and sympathizers.

by Reg Olson 1999

1. Ruth* was born and raised a Methodist. A very bright and talented young girl, she had wanted to be a Methodist minister since childhood. Since she was eight years old she used to line up her stuffed animals in a little 'congregation' and preach to them. Ruth was an honors student in high school and college. She graduated at the head of her seminary class, after completing very successful internships in campus ministry and hospital chaplaincy. At graduation she delivered the baccalaureate sermon, for she

had been chosen by her classmates for this honor. Despite her training, her talents, her wonderful ability to pray, and her gifted preaching ability, she could not become a pastor in her own denomination, for she had realized that she was homosexual (when she was in her twenties) and refused to lie about her identity to the Board of Ordained Ministry. The United Methodist church has lost the leadership of an extremely talented candidate for ministry.

2. George* was a dedicated ministerial candidate. In college he organized various study groups and Christian mission projects. He was the president of his fraternity, which grew and prospered under his leadership. He went on to seminary and honed his skills of leadership and church administration. But when George came up for elders' orders his annual conference made an example of him, discussing his candidacy and voting him out without allowing him to speak or even be present, due to his sexual orientation. The United Methodist Church has lost the skills and dedication of this man's ministry.

3. Bill* was a tall, likeable, blond boy, full of energy and innocence. He went to college and majored in Business Administration, so he could be a financial officer of his denomination, the United Methodist Church. His demeanor led all whom he met to like and respect him, until he told officials of his sexual orientation, and was told that there was no room in the church for him. Although he was working as a highly successful youth minister, his talents were not wanted after he shared his story with his conference. The United Methodist Church has lost the business acumen and Christian dedication of this young man.

4. Sarah* was raised in a Methodist parsonage. She was active in Sunday School and church. An accomplished musical instrumentalist and singer, and a talented organizer, she was elected an officer in her Conference Council on

Youth Ministries during her high school years. After she married, she discovered that she was a lesbian and spent many months agonizing over this new identity.

Although she has grown and matured into a self-confident young Christian woman, Sarah has lost the church that she loved. After searching unsuccessfully for an accepting congregation, she has found a congregation of the United Church of Christ in which she feels accepted and where her talents can be used. The United Methodist Church has lost the musical talents, the educational leadership, and the altruistic dedication of this former United Methodist.

5. Terry* was a "born leader." In high school he was involved in a variety of extracurricular projects, and organized many service projects through his church. He continued to lead his church as a very promising college student, where he was known and respected by all the student body and the faculty. Here was a young man with tremendous skills of communication and organization. Here was a person who could energetically lead the church, for he wanted to be a United Methodist clergyman. But, here was a person who, when he learned of his sexual orientation, was ostracized from the church. The church said it did not need Terry's talents, it did not want HIS enthusiasm

6. Three members of the United Methodist clergy recently joined the United Church of Christ Association in Southwestern Ohio. When asked why they left their denomination they all responded that it was due to the church's stance on the homosexuality issue. It has been said that the United Methodist Church might suffer membership losses over the issue of homosexuality. We need to be aware of the clergy losses that have already occurred! It may be good that United Methodists can share their professional gifts and graces with other churches. It is, however, unfortunate that these clergy are leaving our denomination. They mourn the loss of a church that shaped their moral

and ethical standards, but a church that they say, has moved away from the gospel.

*The names of these persons have been changed to protect them from recriminations and possible attacks from hate-criminals. It is a sorry day when church people have to remain anonymous.

4. Tell Me About The Abomination Of Sodom

I wondered, "What was the real sin of Sodom and Gomorrah?" Then I wrote and distributed this to friends and colleagues.

by Reg Olson 1999

Whenever the topic of homosexuality comes up we hear a lot about the 'sin of Sodom.' It is assumed that the people of Sodom were homosexuals, and that God deemed them to be sinners. Genesis says, 'Their sin is so grievous,' (Genesis 18:20c*), and 'The men of Sodom were wicked and were sinning greatly against the Lord,' (Genesis 13:13). We hear many references to their destruction by the hand of the Lord in Deuteronomy 29:23, Romans 9:29, and Jude 7 which refers to 'suffering the punishment of eternal fire.' Certainly Christians do not want to commit the sins of Sodom and suffer their eternal fate!

But what *was* the sin of Sodom? In Genesis 19 we read of two angels coming to visit Lot in Sodom. Lot implored them to be his guests. He had their feet washed, made them a feast, and gave them hospitality. Then 'All the men, from every part of the city,' came and demanded that Lot bring his guests out 'that we may [know them] have sex with them.' The phrase to *know* is often, although not always, associated with sexual intercourse.

Lot resisted the Sodomites and protected his guests. Then the offenders who were at the door were struck blind (Genesis 19:11). Later, the angels told Lot and his family to leave the city, for they planned to destroy Sodom. They were not to have any second thoughts about it, or "look back," lest they be turned into pillars of salt (like Lot's wife). Then, "The Lord rained down burning sulfur on Sodom and Gomorrah." (Genesis 19:24). One wonders what Gomorrah did to deserve punishment.

Were the men of Sodom homosexuals? If they all were, how did they procreate? If so, why did Lot offer them his two virgin daughters as a substitute for their pleasure** (Genesis 19:8)? Were these men of Sodom living in committed relationships with same sex partners for many years? I doubt that.

Some biblical scholars tell us that the *true* sin of Sodom was their failure to abide by the all-important practice of oriental hospitality. In a rugged environment people are required to practice hospitality to sojourners. The norm of reciprocity dictates that I must welcome you, if, when I am hot, thirsty, hungry, and perhaps lost, I am to expect any hospitality from you. Lot followed this practice to the tee. He implored the angels to rest in his home. The men of the city, however, taunted these strangers to come out and be exposed before them. They were about to violently abuse the angels. This act has more in common with heterosexual rape than with consensual homosexuality in committed relationships!

The prophet Ezekiel spoke of the iniquity of Sodom, and of her sisters Jerusalem and Samaria, (Ezekiel 16: 46 and 48). Did they also practice homosexual acts? Ezekiel says that Sodom had not been as sinful as Jerusalem (Ezekiel 16:48). However, I don't hear the opponents of homosexuality calling for the destruction of Jerusalem! The prophet did catalog the iniquities of Sodom. They were 'arrogant, overfed and unconcerned.' Ezekiel was not opposed to wealth, but the fact that Sodom did not share what she had with the poor and needy, (Ezekiel 16:49)! In other words Sodom was inhospitable! I don't hear the opponents of homosexuality calling for increased charity, welfare rights, or foreign aid!

Nowhere does Jesus, the Son of God, speak of homosexuality, but he does have a word about Sodom. In Luke 19 Jesus commissions the seventy to go out two by two into his harvest. He says that if they are treated with hospitality they should relax and enjoy their welcome. But, he says, if a town does not receive them they should shake the dust of that town off their feet and leave (Luke 10:1-12), for 'it will be more tolerable on that day for Sodom, than for that town.' Jesus is talking about *hospitality*.

If there is a lesson here it may suggest that the United Methodist Church should be more open and accepting of its homosexual offspring. It should welcome them and show them hospitality, and NOT commit the sin of Sodom, by turning them out, by hating them, or by condemning them more than it condemns drunks, gluttons, liars, adulterers, or usurers! Think about it. Perhaps we *should* 'look back' at the story of Sodom, for fear that if we *don't* we might be turned into something worse than pillars of salt. And what is so bad about salt anyway? Jesus said, "You are the salt of the earth," (Matthew. 5:13). "But if salt loses its saltiness, how can it be made salty again? It is fit neither for the soil, nor for the manure pit [dunghill]. It is thrown out. He that has ears to hear, let him hear," (Luke 14: 34-35).

*All biblical references are from the New International Version, Zondervan Publishing House, 1985.

**Lot's daughters were later guilty of having sex with their father in Zoar (ostensibly in order to procreate). The offspring from this union were the Moabites and Ammonites, deemed to be inferior to the Hebrews. We hear nothing today of the "sin of Zoar." Neither is the abomination of incest as popular a topic among biblical conservatives today. I wonder why. I hear no cries to investigate ministerial candidates for a possible history of incest. I know of no crusades against father-daughter incest from the opponents of homosexual holy unions.

5. Ann Arbor Church of the Good Shepherd

Looking for models of church statements of openness we discovered the following written declarations in the bulletin of a church in Ann Arbor

(On the back cover of the bulletin)

Church of the Good Shepherd United Church of Christ

"An interracial, intercultural faith community an open and affirming congregation."

(Inside the bulletin)

Church of the Good Shepherd's Mission Statement

"We, the Church of the Good shepherd, recognize God in our midst and seek to grow in the knowledge of Christ.

"Into God's presence we welcome all who will come, and in our faith community we celebrate the rich diversity of God's people,

"We affirm the worth of each person and strive to nurture each other in love.

"We seek to become a refuge where the walls that divide us are broken down and the wounded find healing.

"We work to make God's realm a reality both in our church and in the larger community."

(on another page)

"The Church of the Good Shepherd United Church of Christ seeks to live and proclaim an active, open-minded, joy-filled faith in Jesus Christ.

“We value inclusive language—the practice of using both masculine and feminine images when referring to humanity and to God. Feel free to use the words you prefer.

“We value racial diversity and seek a style of worship and ministry that reflects the numerous perspectives, traditions, and practices of our diverse ethnic heritage.

“We value and affirm gays, lesbians, and bisexuals, their families and friends, and encourage their full participation in our church’s life and ministry.

“ We value peace and justice, and work to eliminate inequality, prejudice, hate, fear and violence in our community and the world.

“We value the environment and work to restore health to our planet for this and future generations.

“We pray that you will feel welcome among us, and we invite you to assist us in creating new expressions of our common faith and life together.

“May God bless you and your worship here this morning: touch you, heal you, inspire you, challenge you, guide you down new paths in your unfolding journey. May your heart be opened, your mind expanded, and your spirit renewed.”

B. THE NATIONAL CHURCH

"Open the Gates of the Temple"
Hymn by Phoebe Knapp

THE NARRATIVE

The national United Methodist Church had talked about homosexuality as early as 1972, but decided not to press the issue, not to investigate what options laid before it. However, the forces which opposed homosexuality gradually gained ascendancy. As a matter of fact, the Church would go on record in succeeding years to declare that "the practice of homosexuality was incompatible with Christian teaching," that "persons who are openly practicing homosexuals shall not be ordained as clergy," that, "neither our clergy, nor our churches shall be used to celebrate the marriage of homosexuals," and that, "if any organization using funds from the United Methodist Church be found to be fostering the practice of homosexuality, their funding shall be discontinued." The meaning of "fostering the practice of homosexuality" was left to be defined later. The Methodists were not unique in their stance, for the Baptists, Disciples, Presbyterians and Episcopalians held similar positions on these issues.

The United Church of Christ (UCC), one of the more liberal Protestant denominations, had led the way in declaring its willingness to accept candidates for ministry whether they be gay or straight. In 2000 they had even set up a $500,000 scholarship fund for gay and lesbian seminarians. They also urged wider acceptance of homosexuals in the ordained ranks of other denominations. However, the U.C.C. church is congregationally based, with the local church having the ultimate authority to set its own standards for ordination of ministers, and in other matters. We have worshipped in several open and affirming

UCC congregations such as the Good Shepherd United Church of Christ in Ann Arbor Michigan, and Spirit of the Lakes in Minneapolis. But we are also aware that several congregations, in North Carolina and elsewhere, publicly opposed their denomination's position and refused to accept homosexuals as ministers in their churches. Not even the United Churches in Christ are unanimous on the issue of homosexuality. I have heard that out of approximately 6,000 UCC congregations only about 100 have openly homosexual pastors.

Let us reflect on the currents within the church with which my family is a affiliated, the United Methodist Church. In 1988 the General Conference of the United Methodist Church, the international policy-making body of the church, established a Committee to Study Homosexuality, which was charged to report its findings and recommendations to the 1992 General Conference. The committee had a balanced membership of twenty-seven persons, including laity and clergy, administrators at various levels of authority, representatives of theologically conservative, moderate and liberal groups, etc. The committee reported consensus on several issues— that sexuality is God's good gift; that sexual expression is most human when it takes place in the context of a caring and committed relationship; that many gifted homosexuals were within the church; that the causes of homosexuality remained unclear; that it was good to minimize the spread of sexually transmitted disease; that the basic human rights of gays and lesbians should be protected; and that persons of varying opinions on the issue should respect one another. They also agreed the biblical texts on sexuality should be examined in light of their context; that homosexual persons are not universally preoccupied with sex; that they are not prone to seducing others; and that sexual orientation is not deliberately chosen. The committee concluded that, "We do not have to have all of the answers to questions before us in order to keep faith with our profession as Christians. We have had to acknowledge that many of the uncertainties cannot yet be overcome and that many of the perceived certainties cannot be supported. But that may, in itself, have a message for the church. Perhaps we can be less polarized in our discussion on this issue, more humble about our position, and more open to the human realities in our midst." (The Committee to Study Homosexuality Offers the Church ... Its Report, Its Conclusions, Its Recommendations!", Nancy C. Yamasaki, *Circuit Rider, December-January 1991 pages 4-14.)*

The committee recommended the development of a study guide on the issue to be used in local churches. The study guide was balanced and well-written. One wonders how many churches have *ever* used those study materials. How many people have *seen and studied* the curriculum? How *often* has it been used within a local church? Whereas the committee's findings, though not conclusive on all matters, might have contributed to a gradual reconciliation between those opposed to homosexuality and those open to homosexuals, this does not, in fact, seem to have happened.

Three national incidents symbolize the church's continuing polarization on this matter. One was the expulsion of the Oklahoma-based pastor, the Rev. Jimmy Creech, for conducting same-sex weddings, and continuing to do so after being warned that the restrictions against such an act were indeed church law. (The earlier case against him was based on a statement against same-sex weddings made in the *Social Principles of the United Methodist Church.* The question of whether this carried the weight of church law was taken to the Methodist Judicial Council, which ruled that this ruling DID carry the weight of law.) Another was the trial (with Bishop Jack Tuell presiding) and expulsion of the Chicago-based Rev. Greg Dell, for uniting gay members of his congregation in matrimony. And a third event was the corporate celebration of a same-sex union in

California by 68 United Methodist pastors, none of whom was expelled from the church (perhaps because there were too many of them!)

Our family had known at least four young men who had been denied ordination because of their sexual orientation. And there was Rachel, our daughter Liz's partner, who had wanted to become a Methodist preacher from a very early age, but was denied access to ordination. In light of these acts and other similar rejections of gay ministerial candidates Barbara wrote "The United Methodist Church Loses Again," a partial account of our story.

Then an extraordinary thing happened. Bishop Jack Tuell experienced a change of heart, as he received a revelation that God wants us to accept homosexuals and not persecute them. This revelation became the basis of a refreshing breath which blew across the church and gave many of us new heart.

The General Conference of the United Methodist Church 2000 was held in Cleveland, Ohio. Many people hoped that this conference would be more open and affirming to all of God's children. Jeanne Knepper, co-spokesperson for Affirmation: United Methodists for Lesbian, Gay, Bisexual, and Transgendered Concerns, gave a pre-conference address to the press and to heads of annual conference delegations to the General Conference. In it she outlined various hate crimes committed against gays and lesbians, and noted the many ways in which those who perpetrated such crimes did so with a feeling of having the support of the church. She went on to beseech the delegates to "take the barriers [against homosexuals] down."

PFLAG invited parents of homosexuals to come to the conference and make a witness for the inclusion of gays in the church. At the conference we wore badges containing a picture of our gay child, with the motto, "Our child is of sacred worth" emblazoned on it. That statement is taken from the *Book of Discipline*, where it says, "Homosexual persons no less than heterosexual persons are individuals of sacred worth" (section 161 G). However, this same paragraph goes on to say, "Although we do not condone the practice of homosexuality and consider this practice incompatible with Christian teaching, we affirm that God's grace is available to all. We implore families and churches not to reject or condemn their lesbian and gay members and friends."

This paragraph alone highlights the inconsistency of the church on this important issue. Although the national church did not change its position on homosexuality, many persons were affected by our witness, for it pointed out that love and loyalty to children, regardless of their sexual orientation, was a *family value*. Various church leaders congratulated the parents on their presence at the conference.

The events relating to the protest at General Conference were inspiring. The speeches, discussions, and the singing, the forming of a human chain around the conference headquarters, the worship services and the shower of stoles project all left a mark on all participants. The Shower of Stoles project was somewhat reminiscent of the "quilt project" commemorating the victims of AIDS. Clerical stoles of hundreds of ministers who had left churches because of their stance on homosexuality, those denied ordination, those who had suffered abuse and even death, and those representing the churches which had declared themselves to be open and affirming have been gathered to be displayed as a symbol of voices quieted by intolerance. I was so moved by these events that I sat down to write some interpretations of the situation in order to share the spirit of the gathering with other persons. After we left the General conference others, including at least one bishop, committed acts of civil disobedience in opposition to the church's stand. Work to effect national church policy continues between the quadrennial conferences. The battle lines seemed to be drawn, as some vowed to root out the "abomination of homosexuality" from the church, and others called clergy to "stand up and be counted," to "open the gates of the temple" and make their commitment to an open and just church.

We were chagrined, however, to learn that the chances of changing the General Conference's stance on homosexuality were somewhat diminished due to the influence of the churches in other countries. In those areas where the church is growing, there is still a significant degree of protest against granting homosexuals full status similar to that of heterosexuals. This is true in many denominations.

Unfortunately, when the matter of homophobia does spark debate in the larger church the discussion is often camouflaged in theological terms and the word "homosexuality" is not even raised. However, the debate does touch on real issues such as the locus of authority within the church, the question of the need for a creedal basis of uniformity within the church, and the role of debate and reconciliation in the church. These issues relate to the heresy trial of Bishop Joseph Sprague. There were many groups which wanted the church to truly open its doors to all people. Some fear that this issue will permanently divide the church. Others feel that the church must "purify itself" even if it means the loss of membership.

We prayed that opening the gates of the temple would help the Church be truly faithful.

THE DOCUMENTS

1. The United Methodist Church Loses Again

Barbara felt that the church had to hear about the rejection of one of its own children, so she wrote this

piece and asked that it be printed in the church newsletter.

by Barbara, March 25, 2000

The year was 1968. The world was in turmoil as two national leaders, Martin Luther King and Robert Kennedy were assassinated, and the Vietnam War was raging. Amidst all of this chaos, my husband was graduating from Garrett Theological Seminary and being ordained in the Northern Illinois Conference of the Methodist Church.

During this same time a young girl was growing up in Iowa. She grew up as an active member of her United Methodist Church and occasionally practiced "preaching" in the privacy of her bedroom. Her life evolved around a dream of becoming a United Methodist pastor. She was an excellent student, valedictorian of her high school class. She served in an inner-city community center as a US2 mission worker in Ohio. Then she entered Garrett-Evangelical Theological Seminary and continued a tradition of excellence. At her commencement she was chosen by her class to be a commencement preacher. Unfortunately, the story of her plan to be a United Methodist pastor ended there. For, unlike most of her classmates, ordination did not await her. God created her as a lesbian, but the church refuses to believe that God's hand is in this human condition.

This young woman was serving her seminary internship when she met our daughter who was also discovering her sexuality as a lesbian. This was not a choice, but a difficult God-given condition to be embraced. Eventually, these young women forged a truly supportive and loving relationship. They consider one another life partners, and we love both as our daughters. Much to our distress the United Methodist Church has not been there for either of these talented women. They have waited more than ten years for the church to accept all of God's creatures. This has not happened. They have found a home in the United Church of Christ. Both women have worked very successfully in publishing, and they are exceptional daughters, sisters, aunts, friends, neighbors, community members, and caregivers.

The United Methodist Church is not open to such monogamous, talented, contributing persons. Apparently, divorce, adultery, usury, pride, covetousness, abuse, racism, lack of diversity are all more acceptable to the church than an alternate sexual orientation. We choose to alienate gays and lesbians because we feel superior, threatened, and judgmental. We pull a few passages from the Bible to prove our righteous indignation. Never do we place those Biblical passages in the context of a historical period when women were considered chattel and persons were enslaved at the whim of the wealthy. We fail to let God speak to us within the context of our own time. We refuse to hear 'All persons are created in the image of God,' 'God is Love!' or 'Blessed are they who hunger and thirst for righteousness sake for theirs is the Kingdom of God.'

Several months ago the United Church of Christ took our daughter's partner into an 'In Care' status in preparation for ordination. On her local church's recommendation the UCC Association received her as well. She is finally on her way to answering the 'calling' of her God. She will be a wonderful pastor to every congregation she serves. It is indeed sad that we United Methodists have lost her commitment, leadership, and pastoral service. At last summer's United Church of Christ Association meeting in Cincinnati, three United Methodist clergy joined the United Church of Christ due to the United Methodist Church's exclusionary stance on homosexual persons. 'How long, Oh Lord?'

2. Bishop Jack Tuell took a new look at homosexuality, and concluded that the United Methodist stance is wrong.

Many homophobic Christians believe that scripture rejects the practice of homosexuals (the sin of Sodom), and that no reinterpretation of the texts will change the FACT [as they see it] that God opposes homosexuality. In response to this notion of an unchanging God, and an unchanging and reliable interpretation of His Word, retired Bishop Jack Tuell (the same bishop who presided at the trial of Greg Dell) gave this sermon.

United Methodist News Service, March 1, 2000

NEWS OF BISHOP TUELL'S CHANGE OF HEART AFTER THE GREG DELL TRIAL

DES MOINES, WASHINGTON, Feb. 23—Bishop Jack M. Tuell, once an opponent of full ministry with homosexual persons in The United Methodist Church, now says, 'I was wrong.' In a sermon Feb. 20 at his home church in Des Moines, Washington, Bishop Tuell said the tradition of the denomination has not so much actively opposed homosexuality as it has been covering it up. 'As a consequence,' he admitted, 'our real tradition (on this issue) is ignorance.' He declared, however, that the church's longer tradition is that of finally sorting out what is truly important from what is incorrect or marginal. 'In the long run, we have always been able to discern when God is doing a new thing in our midst.' He added: 'This capacity to change is among the noblest of our traditions.' Bishop Tuell explained that his change of heart came after presiding at the church trial of the Rev. Gregory Dell, of Chicago, found guilty of disobeying United Methodist church law by conducting a holy union for two gay men who were active members of his congregation. Of Dell's suspension from exercise of the ministry, Tuell declared: 'Ecclesiastically speaking, the decision was correct. As I understand the Spirit of God, it was wrong.' He evaluated Pastor Dell as 'a dedicated, energetic, compassionate, caring and able minister.' After hearing two days of testimony, Bishop Tuell said, 'I began to see the new thing God is doing' in our church. 'Whatever our beliefs about homosexuality,' Tuell asked, 'can we as Christians do any less than to affirm the mutual commitments of our sisters and brothers in Christ?' In a petition he sent to the General Conference, Bishop Tuell is calling for deleting from church law the recent prohibition against allowing clergy to conduct same-gender holy union services. Bishop Jack M. Tuell, a native of Tacoma, Washington, is both a former attorney and an ordained minister. He served as pastor and district superintendent of United Methodist churches in Washington State, and as bishop in Portland, Oregon, and most recently in Los Angeles. He retired in 1992. He and his wife, Marji, make their home in Des Moines, Washington, a Seattle suburb. (The full text of the sermon follows.)

DOING A NEW THING: The United Methodist Church and Homosexuality

A sermon by Bishop Jack M. Tuell, Des Moines, Washington Preached Sunday, February 20, 2000, at the Des Moines United Methodist Church, Des Moines, Washington

Text: "I am about to do a new thing." —Isaiah 43:19

Religion has never been known as a force at the cutting edge of doing new things. Avant-garde has not been a phrase used to describe the church throughout history rather, the church is usually perceived as a conserving force, seeking to retain the traditional values which have come from the past. This is shown in the respect and honor we give the Holy Bible, a document written several millennia ago. It is seen in the ancient customs of Orthodox Christians, from time honored liturgies to the unchanging clerical vestments of its clergy. Islam thrives on ancient practices such as daily prayers of its people, as five times each day they face toward Mecca. Thousand-year-old statues of the Buddha remain powerful symbols for Buddhists. In Christianity, ancient creeds are recited from week to week in churches around the world.

All of this is good—there is truth and value at the center of religious faith which is unchanging and ought to be honored and revered. John Wesley recognized this in placing tradition as one of four guidelines for us, along with scripture, experience and reason. But our scripture lesson for today reminds us that God is ever ready to do a new thing. It further reminds us that the God we worship is not a static God, capable only of speaking to us from two, three or four thousand years ago. Rather, God is living, alive in this moment, revealing new truth to us here, now, in this year of our Lord 2000. God is revealing new truth in many areas of life. One which is increasingly clear is that God is speaking to us in the issue of homosexuality. I am aware that many people are uncomfortable even mentioning this matter and wish it would just go away. I am aware of that, because I have felt exactly the same way. I am also aware that it is not the most important issue The United Methodist Church faces. The most important issue is to make disciples, to share the love of God in a world that is hurting. But homosexuality is the most volatile and potentially divisive issue we face, and I believe that God is about to do a new thing among us. The new thing that God is doing in our midst right now is to show us that homosexuality is not simply an act or acts of willful disobedience to God's law and commandments, but it is a state of being. It is an identity that God has given to some of His children. It is who they are. How does this assertion—this new thing—stand up against John Wesley's four tests of Christian truth: scripture, tradition, experience and reason?

SCRIPTURE: Twice in the Book of Leviticus and once in the Book of Romans are condemnations of homosexual activity. One in Leviticus indicates that death is the penalty for such acts. In truth, there are instances of homosexual acts which should be condemned, even as there are instances of heterosexual acts which should be condemned. I do not doubt that the writer of Leviticus and that St. Paul had good reason to write as they did. But when we turn to the scripture, we need to turn to the whole of the scripture. When we do that, the central and overwhelming message is God's inclusive love for all of humankind. Scholars of all opinions have agreed that one verse of scripture is truly the 'gospel in a nutshell'— the beloved John 3:16: 'God so loved the world that he gave his only Son that everyone who believes in him may not perish but have eternal life (NRSV).' The overwhelming love of God in Christ sweeps some specific prohibitions away, even though they are in the Bible. Do you believe that? Anyone here divorced? Jesus ruled out almost all divorce. Anyone here a woman? Well, Paul didn't rule you out, but he ruled you out of speaking in church. Anybody here eat pork? Specifically prohibited! Look, the sovereign message of the Bible is God's redeeming, all-powerful love that overrides all else, and places specific prohibitions in the context of the time and place and situation in which they were written.

TRADITION: We remember Tevya in Fiddler on the Roof singing, 'Tradition.' Regarding homosexuality, it is not so much that tradition has been actively against it, but that tradition has been actively covering it up. The tradition is that it is a taboo subject—shrouded in mystery—unspeakable—unmentionable—a subject to be crammed down into the nether regions of our consciousness and forgotten. As a consequence, our real tradition is ignorance. So to that extent, church tradition doesn't help much. In another way, however, we have a long tradition of change. Some 150 years ago, in many of our churches, Methodists believed slavery was scriptural and ordained by God. Until 1920, The Methodist Church in its Discipline prohibited (or tried to prohibit) 'dancing, theater-going, and card-playing.' But we have a long, long tradition of finally sorting out what is truly important over what is either incorrect or only marginally important. In the long run, we have always been able to discern when God is doing a new thing in our midst. This capacity to change is among the noblest of our traditions.

EXPERIENCE: Of all the 4 tests of Christian truth, experience is in some ways the deepest and most far-reaching. It is the thing that can move us when nothing else can. John Wesley was an academic, legalistic, guilt-ridden and slightly repulsive Anglican priest before he experienced the love of God in his heart of hearts—before his heart, as he wrote, was 'strangely warmed.' It turned his life around. It made the difference between his ending up a forgotten cleric of the Church of England and what he is—a man remembered, respected and followed by millions, one of the great spiritual fathers of the human race. What is the role of experience in the issue we speak of today? It is the personal encounter with the anguish, the pain, the hurt, the suffering, the despair which harsh and judgmental attitudes can have on persons of homosexual orientation. How does this encounter come about? One way is when parents realize that their child is a person of homosexual orientation. They share intensely and intimately in the struggle, perhaps the denial, often the anguish, but ultimately the acceptance of the child whom they bore and whom they love. It is little wonder that such parents gather together with others in groups such as PFLAG (Parents, Families and Friends of Lesbians and Gays) to bring about understanding and change. For they have experienced first-hand some of the deep, deep hurt that accompanies this issue in our church and in our society. In my own case, based on my limited understanding, I went along with the prevailing view, although never including any hatred. I said to myself, 'After all, God created men and women different, complementary to one another physically and perhaps emotionally. From my viewpoint as a heterosexual person, heterosexuality must be what God expects of all His creation.' It was just common sense to me. I was wrong. It was experience that showed me I was wrong. Actually, several experiences were at work. A year ago, when Bishop Joseph Sprague of Illinois asked me to come and preside over a church trial, experience made its compelling points with me. The Reverend Gregory Dell was pastor of the Broadway United Methodist Church in Chicago, a congregation made up of about 40% gay and lesbian persons, situated in a community of similar makeup. Under the law of our denomination, Reverend Dell was charged with "disobedience to the order and discipline of The United Methodist Church," for conducting a service of holy union for two members of his congregation, two gay men. These two men were active in their church as ushers, finance committee members, and regular participants. They had been living as partners for several years, but had been having trouble in their relationship. They came seeking spiritual counsel from their pastor, and wanted to have some kind of service of prayer or blessing of their commitment. They felt it would strengthen them and make them better partners. Reverend Dell agreed to conduct a small, informal service, which took place in September of 1998. The facts of the case were never contested. For conducting this service, the trial court found him guilty and suspended him from the exercise of ministry. Ecclesiastically speaking, the decision was correct. As I understand the Spirit of God, it was wrong. For two long days I watched this trial of a dedicated, energetic, compassionate, caring and able minister, with 30 years of loyal service to our church. This experience, along with other experiences I am sure, caused me to change my mind. I began to see the new thing God is doing.

REASON: Reason cuts both ways. For a long time, reason told me that God's creation of male and female ruled out anything but heterosexuality. But reason, enriched by experience, actually told me otherwise. I have often taken issue with arguments which equated prejudice against homosexuality with prejudice against race. I took issue because race was clearly a condition one was born with, while homosexuality involved behavior which is subject to human will. Having said that, is it reasonable to believe that God would create some with an orientation toward the same gender, put within them the same strong drive of sexuality which is present in heterosexual persons, and then decree that such a drive is to be absolutely repressed and denied? This not only defies reason, but is cruel, unfeeling and arbitrary—qualities foreign to God as we know Him in Jesus Christ. Reason supports a belief that God is in the process of doing a new thing. At the trial of Gregory Dell, the two men who were the participants in the service of union appeared as witnesses. On the stand, in response to questions, one man told about his father, a pastor in the Missouri Synod Lutheran Church, one of the most conservative denominations in America. He asked his father to conduct the holy union service. The father regretfully declined, on the basis of his denomination's position, yet he attended the service. Afterwards, at the reception, the father led in a public prayer of blessing for his son and his partner. Whatever our beliefs about homosexuality, can we as Christians do any less than to affirm the committed relationships of our sisters and brothers in Christ? In a few weeks 992 delegates will gather in Cleveland for the General Conference, marking 216 years of our church's life. These are good people, dedicated United Methodist Christians earnestly seeking God's will for our church. They have been elected by their fellow clergy and laity from all over the world and entrusted with a heavy responsibility. They will have differing perspectives on this and many issues facing them. It is impossible to predict what actions they may take, because the Spirit moves at its own pace—'the wind bloweth where it listeth (John 3:8).' But I believe that if the delegates are listening carefully, above the competing pressures of this group and that, they will hear the still, small voice whisper, 'I am doing a new thing,' and they will respond faithfully. Amen.

BIOGRAPHICAL

Bishop Jack M. Tuell is a bishop of The United Methodist Church, now retired. After a brief career as an attorney in Washington State, he joined the Pacific Northwest Annual Conference where he served as a pastor and district superintendent, and was elected three times to the General Conference and four times to the Western Jurisdictional Conference. He was elected to the episcopacy in 1972. He served the Portland Area for eight years, and the Los Angeles Area for 12 years, retiring in 1992. He and his wife, Marji, make their home in Des Moines, Washington. Bishop Tuell was selected to conduct the trial of the Rev. Gregory Dell of Chicago. He had also been asked to be ready to conduct the California-Nevada Annual Conference trial of the Rev. George Fado of Sacramento and the 68 co-officiants of a holy union service. However, the Conference Committee on Investigation chose not to bring the issue to church trial.

3. General Conference of the United Methodist Church May, 2000

Barbara and I felt it was important to share our experiences at General Conference with members of our

congregation, and others.

by Reg Olson, May, 2000

WHY WE WENT TO THE PROTEST GATHERING DURING GENERAL CONFERENCE

We went because we are concerned about the injustices and violence done against homosexuals. We wanted to give a witness to the delegates of our hope that they re-examine the church's stance on the issue of homosexuality. And we went to be supportive of our daughters, and our friends who have been hurt by the church. We were part of the Parents' Reconciling Network (PRN, known in medical circles as 'prescription to be taken as needed'). We wore name badges with pictures of our children and inscription saying, 'My child is of sacred worth' (a quotation taken from the United Methodist book of Discipline). Our group was part of a coalition called AMAR. The 'A' stood for Affirmation: United Methodists for Lesbian, Gay, Bisexual, and Transgendered Concerns. The 'MA' came from the Methodist Federation for Social Action, and the 'R' stood for the Reconciling Congregation Program.

At AMAR's hospitality suite in the Sheraton hotel (across the street from the Convention Center) we saw samples from the Shower of Stoles project clerical stoles of those hurt by the church, who either have left the ministry, entered another denomination, or remained in the closet. We saw the blue silhouettes—one each to honor a homosexual victim of murder or suicide. We examined the literature table, and left two of Barbara's articles, and Reg's comparison between the conversion of Saul/Paul and Bishop Tuell there, as well as distributing them to delegates. We bought a video of the celebrated wedding of Jeannie and Ellie in Sacramento California, done by sixty-eight United

Methodist pastors in January, 1999. Jeannie was on the United Methodist Study Committee on Homosexuality, and was one of only two openly homosexual people who have ever spoken at General Conference. This wedding became the basis of great legalistic controversy. Later we met Jeannie and Ellie and got their autograph of their wedding video tape.

Conferences are a place where we meet old friends and make new ones. We met Terry Sabat, an old friend, now at Breta College. We greeted Greg Dell, the celebrated Chicago pastor who was tried by Bishop Tuell et al. We also met Cindy Bird, formerly of Brighton, and former Program Director of the Christian Center.

We attended the parent's breakfast in the Sheraton on Saturday at 7 AM (after driving 45 minutes to get there). We sat at the table with the Tuells, and Paul Beeman (national chairperson of PFLAG) and his wife Betty, whom we had met in Washington state on July 4 1997. Paul gave a meditation on straining the gnat and swallowing the camel. He spoke of the Exodus of 600,000 Hebrews from Egypt and the 600,000 who have left the United Methodist Church over the issue of Homosexuality. A parent read the 'Statement by the Parents' Reconciling Network.' We were pleased to see others whom we knew at the breakfast, including our bishop.

Later we went to the General Conference session and sat in the visitors' gallery at the Convention Center. We were impressed by the pomp and ceremony, the use of high tech videos, and enthusiastic speakers who talked about new conversions of people by the Korean Church. We thought, 'shouldn't we try to keep some of our gifted homosexual members, and not just discard them?' We left the conference at about 11 AM.

We went to the rally outside the convention center. There we passed out our literature. Barbara passed out 'Hate Hurts, Love Heals' labels. We met and spoke to delegates, most of whom were supportive of an open church. We met visiting Bishops, Craig from Ohio, and others, and listened to Bishop Talbert from California speak. We also heard Bill Johnson, an openly gay clergyman of the UCC, who spoke of his church's opening the doors to diversity many years ago in this same city, Cleveland. And we heard Mel White, Director of Soulforce (who would practice symbolic civil disobedience along with bishops and clergy and laity later in the conference after we left).

We met those who were curious, but not supportive of our quest. It seemed that they all carried their Bibles, many holding them in from of them, as though ready to do an exorcism! We spoke with Japanese delegates, and 'Mark' a pastor from Africa who read from the epistles of Timothy to us, and listened to an AMAR member who told him he had been in a committed gay relationship for 11 years. The gay man quoted scripture back to the pastor, defending his point of view. They seemed to agree that both were children of God, but at their separating, when the gay man tried to shake Mark's hand, Mark recoiled, and said he would not shake! Did he fear that he would get a disease from the gay man? Was he afraid to be seen touching a homosexual? Then I gave our articles to Mark, and I asked him to read about our family's story. Mark asked me if I was a homosexual. I told him I wasn't, but our daughter was a lesbian.

He was very hesitant, but finally took the articles, and shook my hand. He was then approached by two mothers of homosexuals, both in their 60's. He seemed to feel more comfortable with them. They told their story. He asked if they were married (to each other?) One said her husband was dead, and the other said her husband had to work that day. He was pleased with their 'normalcy' and even shook their hands. Later, I went and gave the gay man a hug.

We took communion at the protest podium, and then marched through an arch of multi-colored balloons to the convention hall. As we encircled the Convention Center and extended a multi-colored ribbon around the perimeter, we sang familiar gospel songs, 'It's me, it's me, it's me O Lord,' 'Jesus Loves Me,' 'This little light of mine,' 'Standing on the Promises,' 'We shall overcome,' and 'Oh, How I love Jesus.' As the delegates returning from their lunch break came by, some seemed amused. Some answered me when I greeted them. Others gave stony silent gazes.

That night I couldn't sleep, so I wrote two articles- 'What are we defending?' and 'What is the abomination of Sodom?'

On Sunday we and other protestors worshipped at the First United Methodist Church, Cleveland, at 30th and Euclid. It was a beautiful cathedral type church. All the stoles were there, displayed around the sanctuary, more than 1,000 in number. They had a very impressive Procession of Stoles at the beginning of the service. We had a great two-hour long service, with many illustrious persons present, including Jeanne Audrey Powers, James Lawson of the FOR, who gave the sermon, Mark Bowman of the Reconciling Congregation movement, and the former Rev. Greg Dell.

We left on Monday morning for other meetings in Columbus and Brighton. We prayed for those who would demonstrate on Tuesday and do civil disobedience to call attention to the church's position. One hundred and ninety-one persons were arrested that day, including Bishop Joseph Sprague, Arun Gandhi (nephew of Mohandas Gandhi), James Lawson and others. We wondered, WHAT CAN WE DO?

4. Statement by Parents' Reconciling Network

Supporters of homosexuals, especially parents, can make powerful statements.

Parents' Reconciling Network
May 6, 2000

We are United Methodists who are parents of lesbians, gay men, bisexual or transgendered people (LGBT).

We first came together at a Reconciling Congregations Program gathering in August, 1999. Our purpose: helping others understand that our children are real human beings, not subjects of a vague philosophical issue to be endlessly debated.

Some would have you believe that gay people have no parents.

Mythic figures are made, not born. Too many people believe that GLBT people are fearsome mythological creatures, or subversives whose agenda is to weaken the nation's moral fiber and destroy its churches and families.

There is a reason for this, often unconscious: In order for prejudice to flourish, we must *dehumanize* the victim.

This is true of all prejudice, whether vicious personal hate or the apathetic acceptance of society's institutionalized assumption that only heterosexual life and love are 'normal.'

We as parents know our children are human. How well we know! They are not a vague ethereal 'issue,' whose relationship to God, and the Church can be assessed in terms of discredited clichés and selective distortions of scripture.

When they are unwelcome at worship, the pain is real. When they are tolerated as second-class Christians, the suffering is as real as that of other minorities barred from leadership. When they are told by the actions of church people they are a hell-bound abomination, many believe it—and one-third of adolescent suicides are GLBT teens.

Officially we deny them any of the support in long-term loving relationships that we lavish on non-gay couples. Then we criticize what we perceive as promiscuity.

In the end, many turn their backs in sorrow and in anger.

That's why we wear the badge. That's why we tell their stories to all who will listen: to set the record straight.

A second thing happens to the majority population when our LGBT brothers and sisters are dehumanized. Most non-gays are unable to *hear* them.

Just as with other minorities, society and the Church turn for their information to some of the people least likely to know.

It is astounding but true: In the 28 years of debate over LGBTs in the United Methodist Church, *only two* openly gay people have been heard from the stage of the General Conference!

The problem for the Church, despite our refusal to see it, is very real. We do not practice the grace we profess.

Example: At the 2000 General Conference, a commendable media campaign is being proposed that would say, 'All are welcome in the UMC' —while well-organized caucuses work successfully to make just the opposite true.

Example: Our Discipline proclaims, 'Homosexual persons [are] of sacred worth,' while the 1992 General Conference roundly rejected the conclusion of its own Study Committee: that there is 'insufficient evidence to sustain' the derogatory assertion that living as LGBTs was 'inconsistent with Christian teaching.'

Example: We proclaim repentance for racial wrongs. But many question how meaningful these can be when parallel wrongs—including those done to our gay children—still find their justification in the Church. Repentance without reconciliation is cheap grace.

As parents, the only answer that works with our children is unconditional love. The idea is at the heart of our faith, and its name is 'grace.'

It has a model for grace, and his name is Jesus, the Christ.

We commend this model. No: as faithful members of the United Methodist Church, we *demand* a return by our Church to this model: The loving Christ, whose *commandment*— not an elective, but a requirement — was loving God with all our hearts, and loving our neighbors as ourselves.

We are your neighbors in the pews, and so are many of our children. It is time to recover this great lost treasure for the church, by living the commandment.

5. Christianity and Homosexuality

After attending the solidarity events at General Conference I felt inspired to write and distribute the following essay.

by Reg Olson, April 4, 2000

'All of them condemned him.'

Two scripture lessons I heard this Sunday stand out to me. The first, from Mark 14: 63, pertained to the 'trial' of Jesus before the high priest of Jerusalem. It read in part, 'All of them condemned him.' The authorities found Jesus guilty of their charges and they prepared for his crucifixion.

It seems to me that this is how the homosexual might feel in the Christian church today. When one of my daughters told me that gays and lesbians have difficulty 'coming out' to their family and friends, but that it is even more difficult to 'come out Christian' to friends in the gay and lesbian community her words struck a cord in my heart. Why should a person find it embarrassing to publicly declare that they are Christian (unless they are in some kind of totalitarian state which is against religion)?

'All of them condemned him,' is a common experience of a homosexual who asks, 'what is the attitude of the Church toward a person like me?' I would like to suggest that this is the wrong perception of the Christian church! There are some groups whose theology makes it necessary to condemn the actions of a homosexual. Most of the more fundamental groups do this. But there are also groups, such as the Unitarian-Universalists, most Quakers, many United Church of Christ members, a lot of Episcopalians, and most recently the Reform Rabbinate of Judaism which are open and accepting of a homosexual to the point of welcoming them, baptizing and marrying them, and perhaps welcoming them into the priesthood. There are many other 'mainline' Protestant groups, such as my own United Methodist Church, the Presbyterians, Disciples, Baptists etc. who are deeply divided over the issue of the alleged 'sin of Sodom and Gomorrah.' Some of the members and leaders of these churches support the marriage or union of homosexuals in a committed relationship, and even support the ordination of gay and lesbian clergy candidates. So I would like to declare that many Christians are in open support of homosexual rights (and many others are still in the closet on this matter.) We do not condemn you!

Release to the Captives

The second scriptural passage I heard this weekend is the phrase that describes the ministry of Jesus (Luke 4:18) in light of the Old Testament Suffering Servant passage (Isaiah 61:1-2) and says that Jesus came to proclaim 'release to the captives.' It seems to me that this is the good news of Christianity to gays and lesbians who have been 'captured' by theologies and political agendas today.

We can be released from the notion that 'All of them condemned him.' The churches are not universal in their rejection. (Why do I say 'we can be released?' It is because even those of us who are heterosexuals are in bondage to the same ideologies which bind homosexuals.)

We can be released from the stereotypes about Gays and Lesbians that suggest they are all promiscuous, child-molesting people in drag. The data tells us that gays in a committed relationship are likely to be more faithful than heterosexual couples, and that lesbian couples are the most faithful. Far from being violent as a group, homosexuals are more likely to be victimized, as Matthew Sheppard was, to suffer from 'gay bashing' often perpetrated by people who have some vague notion that God hates gays! We need to be released from the notion that all homosexuals have 'chosen' their sexual orientation. An increasing body of research points to a biological, genetic basis for homosexuality. Perhaps homosexuals did not 'choose' their sexual orientation any more than I, a heterosexual, did!

We can be released from the silence which condones homophobia. I say **homophobia**, because there seems to be a deep-seated fear among us of homosexuality and homosexuals. Is it because of scriptural texts condemning 'sodomy?' Is it because of an ideology of male superiority which seems threatened by the specter of males and females 'performing unnaturally?' Is it due to a fear that the human race will forget how to propagate if homosexuality is permitted?

I do not believe that the Bible condemns homosexuality

I think that the Bible doesn't even talk about

homosexuality as a lifestyle as we know it today. It wasn't a lifestyle that the Old Testament was considering in Genesis 18. Sodom and Gomorrah were guilty not of homosexuality, but of **violence and gross inhospitality**. They violently humiliated others by an act of gang rape!

In support of this assertion we might ask what other scriptural references to the 'sin of Sodom' say. Ezekiel 16 says that the real sin of the people of Sodom was their abundance of material goods, and their failure to meet the needs of the poor. In Luke 10 Jesus says that Sodom and Gomorrah will be treated more kindly than any city that mistreats and rejects his disciples (again a hospitality issue)

'How did we come to reject homosexuals?' they ask? 'Where does homosexuality appear in the 10 commandments?' *Nowhere!* 'or in the Sermon on the Mount?' N*owhere.* Other passages are understood by some Christians to be speaking of foreign religious practices, or of a culture bound assertion of male supremacy! While many verses can **be used to support homophobia** it might be concluded that, "The Bible says as much directly about homosexuality as it does about the Internet!'

Theologian Walter Wink, of Auburn Seminary, raises the interesting question of WHICH sexual ethic from the Bible should the Christian follow today?

He notes that there are several sexual practices which **we almost universally condemn** today which are **encouraged** in the Bible. These include the levirate marriage, taking of concubines, prostitution, polygamy, treating women as property, etc.

He says there are some practices which are **discouraged** in the Bible, but which **society seems to accept** today, such as a display of nudity to one's spouse, birth control, naming sexual organs, celibacy, and divorce, etc.

He notes that there are several practices named in the Bible with which Christians are in full agreement, such as the rejection of incest, rape, adultery, intercourse with animals, etc.

In short, according to one theologian, the Bible does not speak with one voice on sexual ethics!

Even if homosexuality were a sin, 'God can forgive,' many Christians say today. What makes it worse than divorce, gluttony, lying, adultery, stealing, murder, drunkenness and usury? Why is it such a special sin?

Why does the United Methodist *Discipline* say more about homosexuality than the New Testament does? (and perhaps more than the whole Bible does?)

We can be released

We can be free from the exclusiveness of the churches which says that homosexuals can go to church, be baptized, etc., but they cannot be united into holy matrimony, and cannot serve as clergy (ministers and priests).

Let me share a brief description of what has been going on in one of the largest denominations in the nation, the United Methodist church.

The rule book of the United Methodist Church, the *Discipline* says that 'homosexuals are people of sacred worth' also has paragraph supporting the civil rights of gays and lesbians.[5] BUT it also says, 'Ceremonies that celebrate homosexual unions shall not be conducted by United Methodist ministers.' 'Self-avowed practicing homosexuals are not to be ordained as ministers.'

In 1997 Omaha pastor, The Rev. Jimmy Creech was charged with performing a union ceremony for two men. He was ultimately acquitted of the charge because the prohibition against homosexual unions was not deemed to be part of church law.

In August, 1998 the Judicial Council, the highest court in the Church, ruled that the United Methodist Social

Principles' statement against such unions has the weight of church law.

March 26, 1999 Greg Dell was removed from his ministry for presiding at a same sex union in Chicago, after a trial conducted by the national church, with retired bishop Jack Tuell presiding.

Sixty-nine United Methodist ministers together celebrated a holy union of two women in Sacramento California on January 16, 1999. But the charges against them were dismissed calling forth a response from the **Conservative** Coalition for United Methodist Accountability which said they should have been tried. The Good News coalition wants a strong reaffirmation of the Discipline. It wants to send a signal across the church that we are really serious about this. The Confessing Movement wants General Conference to reinforce the Discipline's language dealing with the church's position on homosexuality. It also wants to include same sex unions under the chargeable offenses against an errant preacher. [6.7.]

On the other side of the issue there is the **Progressive** coalition consisting of Affirmation, the Methodist Federation for Social Action, and the Reconciling Congregation's Program. They want to remove the language which describes homosexuality as 'incompatible with Christian teaching.' They would also allow same sex unions for those in a committed relationship and the ordination of all qualified candidates without consideration of sexual orientation.

Most recently United Methodist **Bishop Jack Tuell** (who presided at the trial of Greg Dell) repented of his position in a sermon in which he said, 'I was wrong!' Taking his text from Isaiah 43:19 'I am about to do a new thing.' The Bishop said that God is revealing new truth to us about homosexuality. [See Bishop Tuell's position on pages 65 and following, above.]

Both sides think they are right, that they speak for God on this issue. In the days preceding the American Civil

War the Methodist church split into the old Methodist Episcopal Church North and the Methodist Episcopal Church South over the issue of slavery. That split was finally healed in 1939 when the former churches reunited. One wonders if there is any way to prevent a split today, or if the church should split in order to be faithful!

In his home town Jesus read from Isaiah 61:1-2, saying, 'The spirit of the Lord is upon me because he has anointed me; he has sent me to announce good news to the poor, to proclaim release for prisoners, and recovery of sight for the blind; to let the broken victims go free, to proclaim the year of the Lord's favour.' (Luke 4:18-19 NEB) Is the year 2000 the year of the Lord's favor for the United Methodist Church?

6. Why are church persons so opposed to homosexuality?

Recognizing that some church people who are so vehemently opposed to homosexuality must have some reason for their strong feelings, I wrote the following to stimulate thought and discussion.

by Reg, 2000

WHY ARE CHURCH PERSONS SO OPPOSED TO HOMOSEXUALITY? WHY IS IT PLACED ABOVE ALL OTHER "TRANSGRESSIONS?"

Here are some possible reasons why some people are so opposed to homosexuality. Which do you think is most plausible? Is it because of...

1. The natural law argument—that procreation is needed, and that 'animals don't do it' (it, meaning homosexual behavior)

2. The personal fear of being contaminated by 'homosexual sinners'

3. The personal guilt for having homosexual impulses

4. The acceptance of stereotypes—pederasty, promiscuity, violent behavior, and drug use among homosexuals

5. The lack of information—ignorance about real GLBT persons

6. The dogmatic reading of the Bible—failure to examine alternative interpretations,

7. The need to preserve male dominance

8. The authoritarian personality (as on racism, sexism, etc.)

9. The fear of suffering like the people of Sodom

10. A shroud of secrecy 'don't talk about it'

11. The view that 'we never met a homosexual'

12. The belief that homosexuals want recruits (that recruits get a free toaster ovens!)

13. The belief that it is all a matter of choice

14. The need to find scapegoats for personal or social problems

Are there other reasons?

7. Two days of civil disobedience stun United Methodists. 218 arrested demanding justice for sexual minorities

After our experience at the General Conference in Cleveland we returned to our home and our daily routines. We learned that the forces of reconciliation were even more assertive at the conference after we had left.

Tuesday, May 16, 2000, by Laura Montgomery Rutt, Director of Communications for Soulforce, Inc.

SOULFORCE NEWS ALERT

Gandhi, King, Civil Rights Heroes and United Methodist Bishops Launch Soulforce Campaign to End "Holy War" Against Homosexuals. Soulforce Announces Plans for Presbyterian and Episcopalian Events

CLEVELAND (May 13, 2000) Discriminatory policies against sexual minorities in the United Methodist Church resulted in 191 arrests, May 10, and 27 arrests, May 11, for acts of civil disobedience at the General Conference of the nation's second largest Christian denomination in Cleveland, Ohio. Those arrested included United Methodist Bishop C. Joseph Sprague Northern Illinois) and Bishop Susan Morrison Northern New York), civil right leaders from the '50s and '60s, members and clergy of The United Methodist Church, and Soulforce activists from 24 states. It also marked a first arrest for Arun Gandhi, grandson of Mohandas Gandhi, who traveled to Cleveland to help launch the ecumenical, interfaith Soulforce campaign to end the 'holy war' against homosexuals being waged by Catholic, Protestant, and Mormon churches.

The May 10 civil disobedience coincided with an ecumenical worship service addressed by the (Anglican) Archbishop of Canterbury and attended by 5,000 United Methodists and heads of 20 other denominations with anti-homosexual policies in place. The arrest of 191 people of faith continued for ninety minutes as a dozen different Soulforce 'Prayer Squads' blocked the exit from the Cleveland Convention Center in a Silent Vigil carrying signs that read 'No exit without justice.' Hundreds of supporters sang hymns and applauded as each 'squad' was arrested. Nearby, anti-gay protestors shouted obscenities and waved signs reading 'God Hates Fags' and 'Got AIDS Yet.' Officials from the Cleveland Mayor's Office and Police commended the large Soulforce delegation for their disciplined and peaceful act of civil disobedience.

‘For three decades Catholic and Protestant leaders have debated our issue,’ explained Dr. Mel White, Soulforce Founder and the last person to be arrested. ‘Each debate ends with another act of injustice. They’ve declared our lives ‘incompatible with Christian teaching.’ They’ve refused to ordain us for ministry, to bless our loving relationships, or to budget funds for programs that assist or welcome our sisters and brothers. We’re blocking this exit to say to the 1,000 Methodist delegates and their ecumenical guests, ‘This debate is over. The suffering has gone on too long. Stay in there this time until you do justice. And if you don’t, we give you fair warning that we love the church too much to stand by in silence. We are launching a plan today in the loving, nonviolent spirit of Jesus, Gandhi, and King that will demonstrate our determination to end the injustice forever.’

The 191 Soulforce delegates who were arrested spent the day in jails across Cleveland. They were fingerprinted and photographed. Some were handcuffed. By evening, each person had appeared before a local judge to pay a $155 fine. Soulforce activists paid almost $30,000 in fines and court costs to take this stand for justice. Thursday, May 11, when the delegates voted to maintain their anti-homosexual policies twenty-seven United Methodist leaders were arrested the second time after staging a Pray-In on the stage of the Convention Center.

At a press conference and debriefing held Thursday, May 11, Greg Marlan and Karen Weldin, Co-Chairs for the Soulforce action in Cleveland, joined Dr. White to announce - RELIGHT THE FLAME - a four-year Soulforce strategy to help end discrimination against sexual minorities by the United Methodist Church. Soulforce will be working for justice at the upcoming Presbyterian and Episcopal Conventions later this summer.

ABOUT SOULFORCE: Soulforce (www.soulforce.org) is an ecumenical, interfaith coalition dedicated to applying the principles of relentless nonviolence as taught by Gandhi and King on behalf of all who suffer injustice, especially sexual minorities.

CONTACT: Dr. Mel White, (949) 455-0999 or RevMel@aol.com

8. Statement of Clergy Commitment

Attempts have been made to involve greater numbers of United Methodist Clergy in opposing their church's official stand on homosexuals.

by the Proclaiming the Vision Committee
January 15, 1997

The purpose of this statement is 'to be a clear, unequivocal, public statement that holy unions for all persons, regardless of gender, are being celebrated and will continue to be celebrated, privately and publicly.' Signed copies are being sent to Affirmation and to District Superintendents and Bishops of the United Methodist Church. Sent out by the 'Proclaiming the Vision Committee,' the statement reads:

'We, the undersigned clergy of the United Methodist Church, have watched for many years as General Conference actions have added increasingly condemnatory and exclusionary language to the Book of Discipline concerning the full participation of gay and lesbian persons in our denomination. The 1996 General Conference added the words, 'Ceremonies that celebrate homosexual unions shall not be conducted by our ministers and shall not be conducted in our churches,' (paragraph 65.C) to the Social Principles of the church.

'We understand the Social Principles to be instructive and legally non-binding. Nevertheless, we recognize the directive tone of this addition and make public our opposition to it by declaring that we will not be bound by it.

'We reaffirm the statement contained within the 'In All Things Charity' document, 'To withhold rituals of support and accountability for committed relationships is unconscionable. The standards for preparation and celebration of [covenantal unions] with same-gendered couples should be the same as for weddings of heterosexual couples.'

'We publicly state that we will celebrate rites of union with all couples, regardless of gender, as part of the pastoral responsibilities consistent with the gospel and spirit of Jesus Christ, entrusted to us by the United Methodist Church'.

9. The trial of Bishop Joseph Sprague

The heresy trial of Bishop Joseph Sprague raises issues of authority, belief and reconciliation.

From "NewsDesk" Tues, 18 Feb 2003. A UMNS Report By Kathy L. Gilbert, news writer for United Methodist News Service, Nashville, Tenn. (615) 742-5470

COMPLAINTS DISMISSED AGAINST BISHOP JOSEPH SPRAGUE

United Methodist Bishop Bruce B. Ough, president of the church's North Central Jurisdiction College of Bishops, has announced that complaints filed against Bishop C. Joseph Sprague of Chicago have been dismissed. A four-person supervisory response team met in January and February to review the complaints and respond to them.

A group of 28 United Methodist clergy and laypeople filed the complaint against Sprague on Dec. 30, calling for his removal based on comments that he made about Christ's divinity at a speech at Iliff Theological Seminary and in his book *Affirmations of a Dissenter*.

[After the trial] they said, 'We affirm the supervisory team's recommendations for theological dialogue and declare our willingness to participate. We believe, however, that we as a church need to go beyond dialogue to develop an understanding of what binds us together theologically in the United Methodist Church--what our theological identity is. This decision appears to give official sanction to the personal interpretation of our doctrinal standards in a way that diminishes their unifying and binding force. Sadly, this approach to theology within the United Methodist Church will only deepen our divisions and weaken the mission and ministry of our church. ...'

Sprague released a public statement Feb. 13. 'It was my intent, in the Iliff lecture and with the book, to stimulate informed debate,' he said. 'It was not my intent that those who were unaware of the issues raised would be confused or hurt.'

Sprague also points to Paragraph 104 [of the *Discipline*,] which states in part that the theological task of United Methodists is the 'testing, renewal, elaboration, and application of our doctrinal perspective in carrying out our calling to spread spiritual holiness over the lands. The Iliff lecture, the book, my preaching, teaching and other writings reflect an unequivocal commitment to both honoring and interpreting Scripture and tradition,' Sprague said. 'As a bishop, I shall continue to guard, interpret, live and transmit the wondrous treasure we have been given, in earthenware vessels, until that time when I no longer see through a glass darkly but face to face.'

[The Supervisory Response Team said,] "The statement further states this matter is an opportunity for the church to 'seek the Spirit's wisdom.' The church's mission is being diminished in part because of factions in the denomination that do not listen or talk to one another across theological lines.

Let us enter into a season of listening deeply to the Holy Spirit and to one another. Let us cast out our penchant to power and control. Let us lay aside our arrogance. Let us reclaim our mission of 'spreading scriptural holiness across the land ...'

In response to a question about the unity of the Christian witness at a recent ecumenical gathering in Columbus, Ohio, Dr. James Forbes, pastor of New York's Riverside Church, said, 'When we recognize the common threat, we will come together.' Many in our Church believe the threat is doctrinal impurity and heresy. Others in our Church believe the threat is the narrowing of Wesleyan doctrine to a static, rigid formulation. It is the humble, but considered, opinion of the supervisory response team that the real threat may well be our arrogance and parochial attitudes. The Evil One is surely enjoying our folly!'

[Bishop Ough noted that,] 'Only surrender to Christ Jesus will move us beyond our addiction to schismatic attitudes and litigious behaviors and toward the unity of mission we profess, but do not practice. Only a deep, abiding, persistent listening to the Holy Spirit will remind us of what Christ would have us be and do.

'We conclude with Jesus' words from his farewell conversation with the twelve disciples: 'But the Advocate, the Holy Spirit, whom the Father will send in my name, will teach you everything, and remind you of all that I have said to you. Peace I leave with you; my peace I give to you. I do not give to you as the world gives. Do not let your hearts be troubled, and do not let them be afraid. You heard me say to you, 'I am going away, and I am coming to you.' If you love me, you would rejoice that I am going to the Father, because the Father is greater than I. And now I have told you this before it occurs, so that when it does occur, you may believe. I will no longer talk much with you, for the ruler of this world is coming. He has no power over me; but I do as the Father has commanded me, so that the world may know that I love the Father. Rise, let us be on our way.' (John 14:26-31, NRSV)

'Indeed, Church, rise, let us be on our way. Let us not miss this opportunity. Let us enter into a season of listening deeply to the Holy Spirit and to one another. Let us cast out our penchant to power and control. Let us lay aside our arrogance. Let us reclaim our mission of 'spreading scriptural holiness over the lands.'

'In the name of Jesus Christ, let us rise up and be on our way!'

Bishop Bruce R. Ough, President North Central Jurisdiction College of Bishops for the Supervisory Response Team.

C. ANNUAL CONFERENCE JUNE, 2000 BACK TO REGIONAL REALITIES

"Surely the Lord is in This Place, and I Did Not Know It."
(Gen. 28:16b RSV)

THE NARRATIVE

Returning from the exhilarating experience of the protest at General Conference, we faced the realties of homophobia in the real world. One of the dangers of attending protest gatherings is that we sometimes lose sight of the fact that we are in a minority. It is comforting to know that there are others who have similar convictions, but we cannot stay at the party forever.

At our annual conference in Lakeside a few of us supplied some informational papers and flyers to the Reconciling United Methodists' (RUMS) display table in the Soul Café exhibit area. I was surprised to see one particular piece of literature on the table. Here is the story behind that surprise. At the clergy session of our Annual Conference of West Ohio United Methodists a question was raised about the status of a candidate for ordination. It was noted that he was an open homosexual, and had been forthcoming to his district superintendent and the bishop about this. Many people spoke on his behalf, saying that he had the gifts and graces to become an excellent minister. Unfortunately the *Methodist Discipline* said he could not be ordained! One proponent of "fairness and reconciliation" stated that perhaps the candidate could vow to remain celibate, and not **practice** homosexuality. If he could do so, he might meet the letter of the law. I stood up at that point and asked how many of the heterosexual ministers would be willing to consider taking that vow themselves!

The bishop said that the conference could make its own decision on this matter, and did not have to defer to the *Discipline*, so the clergy had a standing vote on the issue.

I stood with the minority who upheld the principle of openness and affirmation of the candidate. This whole discussion and action was a confidential matter, and we were admonished not to speak to the media about it afterwards. I was surprised later, when at the full session of the annual conference, I saw some literature describing this event and conference decision. When I said that it might be inappropriate to have this literature available for all to see I was told that the complete story was already told in the Columbus newspaper the night after the clergy session! So much for confidentiality!

During the conference there was an exceptional opportunity to have dialogue in mixed groups of persons with varying theologies. The dialogue groups were intentional gatherings established to promote mutual understanding and respect among delegates who might not otherwise listen to each other, due to their opposing views. The groups were allowed to pick any controversial topic they wanted to discuss. Many chose the church's position on homosexuality. In my group there seemed to be a fair amount of openness and acceptance of differences of opinion. This was made possible because the ground rules specified how we were to interact. However, when the full conference reconvened, many people took the "party line" and spoke as members of interest groups who were for or against various issues. Sociologists speak of "reference groups" to designate the effect those who are important to us have on our opinions and actions. I wondered, "When will the reference group of church people include a *mixture* of gays and straights, singing and fellowshipping together?"

The annual conference did not overturn the church's official stances on homosexuality. We were not surprised at this. During the period when the candidates for ordination were being presented to the annual conference I joined a large group of Reconciling United Methodists who ringed the auditorium in silent protest of the fact that ordination was not available to homosexual candidates. Each of us held in our hands one of the stoles which had been dedicated to the Shower of Stoles Project, as a symbol of an unaccepted ministry. We held them high, as if to say, "but what of these children of God? Can't they be accepted into ministry?"

This was Bishop Craig's last conference, as she was about to retire as bishop. She told the conferees that this gave her special privilege, as she could say things that a sitting bishop could not normally say. And so she gave us admonitions to be more open and accepting, to love one another, and not be moved by hatred. Some people were visibly moved and appreciated her courage, but others were moved to express their dislike for her "audacity." They should not have been surprised, as our bishop was one of only fifteen who had made a public declaration at the General Conference of 1996, in Louisville, that the church was not of one mind on the issue of homosexuality. They said that silence had prevailed too long among the bishops, and that the time had come to say they disagreed with the church's official stance. Our bishop, and others as well, were to suffer greatly for this courageous act, as conservative church men and women would let her know of their displeasure with her stance, withhold their contributions to the church in protest, and withdraw from the church all together (as well as threatening to take even more radical actions).

Other annual conferences have defunded organizations they had formerly sponsored under the *Discipline*'s rubric that no agency receiving United Methodist funds shall promote homosexuality. (806.9 General Council on Finance and Administration—"It shall be responsible for ensuring that no board, agency, committee, commission, or council shall give United Methodist funds to any gay caucus or group, or otherwise use such funds to promote the acceptance of homosexuality. The council shall have the right to stop such expenditures.") The Virginia Annual Conference used that standard to withdraw their funds from an ecumenical campus ministry. At the West Ohio Board of Higher Education meeting on funding allocations a minority voted to terminate support for a university because they had "gay ministry." "Even if our money doesn't go to support that ministry it will free up other money to do so," they said. I responded saying, "Who are we to tell other funding groups what they can do? If, for instance, the United Church of Christ asked a pastor of an ecumenical campus ministry to reach out to gays and lesbians we would not have the right to prevent that ministry from taking place." Churches' varying rules about homosexuality constitute a barrier to true ecumenical unity.

We prayed that all churches could come to feel the presence of a loving and forgiving God.

THE DOCUMENTS

1. How can Christians defend homosexuals?

We had literature displayed at the "Soul Café" for a second year at the Annual Conference.
I wrote this essay for distribution at the conference.

by Reg Olson, 2001

Many believers wonder how Christians could, in good conscience, defend an "abomination" as great as homosexuality. Are such defenders committing as great a sin by their defense of homosexuality? In order to better understand the actions of bishops, clerics, laymen and laywomen who participate in the struggle against homophobia* we need to be clear about what they are *not* attempting to defend.

1. We are not defending sexual violence, abuse, or rape, whether it be homosexual or heterosexual.

2. We are not trying to defend casual sex, or promiscuity, or adultery whether it be homosexual or heterosexual.

3. We are not supporting pederasty, or sex between adults and children. That is not the same thing as homosexuality.

4. We are not defending the use of drugs.

5. We are not promoting group sex.

6. We do not defend attempts of persons to force their sexuality upon others, as a "better alternative."

7. We do not uphold pornography.

"What do we defend or uphold?

8. We uphold the gift of sexual identity at birth, a gift of God's creation, whether it be homosexual or heterosexual.

9. We appreciate the gift of sexual relationships, which are not just limited to procreation.

10. We uphold heterosexual procreation, as part of God's injunction 'to be fruitful and multiply.'

11. We support faithful, committed sexual relationships, whether they be homosexual or heterosexual.

12. We uphold the sacredness of family relationships, whether they be homosexual or heterosexual.

13. We defend the right of persons to be safe and secure from the violence of physical force, words or ideology.

14. We support the church's defense of all persons, regardless of their age, race, gender, nationality, ethnicity, social class, education, or sexual orientation. Truly we are the family of God!

Christians have a great deal of common ground regardless of their stance on this potentially divisive subject.

* We use the term "homophobia" because of the association of homosexuality with the behaviors listed above in 1-7."

2. News about Phil Hart

A very dramatic event occurred at the clergy session of the annual conference. Here is the news report on the event.

June 1, 2000 by United Methodist News Service

UNITED METHODISTS DISMISS OHIO PASTOR

A United Methodist pastor from Ohio has been dismissed from the ministry because of his sexual orientation. In a May 31 executive session, clergy members of the West Ohio Annual (regional) Conference voted to discontinue 30-year-old Phil Hart from probationary membership. He was a 'deacon probationary member' and had not yet achieved final status as an elder with full connection to the church.

Hart, who works for a social service agency in Franklin County, was ordained in 1996 but told church officials later in 1998 that he is homosexual and cannot promise to remain celibate. The United Methodist *Book of Discipline* has defined the practice of homosexuality as being 'incompatible with Christian teaching' and states 'self-avowed practicing homosexuals are not to be accepted as candidates, ordained as ministers or appointed to serve in the United Methodist Church.'

The Rev. Tom Slack, editor of the West Ohio Conference newspaper, said the vote to dismiss Hart was not unanimous but that no vote count had been released. Four other probationary members also were discontinued. One had died, two others had decided to join other denominations, and a fourth had exceeded the time limit for the probationary period.

A native of Columbus, Ohio, Hart is a lifelong United Methodist and graduate of Asbury Theological Seminary in Kentucky. Currently finishing work on a master's degree in communications, he served eight years as a pastor in local churches and taught theology for two years at Circleville College. Last November, Hart was one of six 'witnesses' in a conversation on homosexuality sponsored by the United Methodist Commission on Christian Unity and Interreligious Concerns. During that discussion, he shared experiences about both his childhood calling to the ministry and his growing self-loathing about his attraction to men, even to the point of contemplating suicide. At the age of 27, he said then, he finally decided to accept himself as he was.

3. Money talks

We must not forget that there are people who strongly resent the presence of homosexuals in the church and its programs. Here is a story which gives cause to ponder to any campus ministry that wants to make a witness for reconciliation.

by Ruth McMurtrie, *Chronicle of Higher Education*, February 2, 2001

Methodists Pull Funds From Group That Accepted Gay Students

The United Methodist Church in Virginia has decided to stop financing an interdenominational Christian group at Mary Washington College after the head of the church's higher-education-ministries board concluded that the group is too accepting of gay and lesbian students.

Mary Washington's Campus Christian Community, which has been run jointly by Lutherans, Presbyterians, Episcopalians, and United Methodists since 1972, has wrestled with the Virginia Annual Conference of the United Methodist Church's Board of Higher Education Ministries for two years over the issue of homosexuality. Some United Methodist students and community members complained that the campus group, which is housed in a building owned by the Virginia Methodist conference, has become dominated by gay and lesbian students in recent years. Gay students, in turn, said they simply want to be accepted for who they are.

Last month, the church's college-ministries board informed the Christian group that it would start its own campus ministry at the Fredericksburg institution in July, and that it would end its support for the Campus Christian Community at that time. It also decided to take back the building, leaving the Christian group without a home. The United Methodist board currently contributes $55,000 to the Christian community's $103,000 annual budget.

Catherine Walker, chairman of the Campus Christian Community board and a United Methodist, said she was 'devastated.' She defended the group against charges that it promotes homosexuality because it welcomes gay students. 'We are not advocating any special group,' she said. 'However, we are inclusive, and we do say: 'Come, journey with us. We want you to feel safe and comfortable here.'

An Inclusive Ministry

Tensions began during the tenure of the previous Campus Christian Community pastor, the Rev. Daphne Burt, a Lutheran. Pastor Burt, who left in December 1999 for a job at the University of Chicago, made gay students a part of her ministry. She even performed a gay union ceremony.

The higher-education-ministries board began relaying its concerns to the board of the Christian community in 1999 and halted a search for Pastor Burt's successor over concerns about the group's direction.

Ms. Walker said her board tried to allay the fears of the United Methodists. Of particular concern was a certificate given to the Christian community by a Lutheran organization stating that the community was a member of its Reconciled in Christ program. The program recognizes congregations that welcome lesbians and gay men.

Ms. Walker said that the certificate was sent by the Lutheran group in response to a vigil that Christian community members held for Matthew Shepard, a gay student at the University of Wyoming who was beaten to death. She said that the Campus Christian Community had never applied for membership in the program. But Elizabeth Neidig, a junior, said that student members of the Christian community had in fact applied for Reconciled in Christ standing long before the vigil took place.

Whatever the origin of the certificate, the Christian community's board agreed that it would not formally apply to become a member of Reconciled in Christ. It did, however, amend its mission statement to say that it welcomed students regardless of sexual orientation.

The United Methodist board apparently felt that the group had not distanced itself enough from programs that support gay people. In November, Ms. Walker received a letter from Ira L. Andrews III, president of the Virginia Conference Board of Higher Education Ministries and dean of students at Randolph Macon College. Mr. Andrews wrote that the Campus Christian Community's focus on gay men and lesbians was 'of grave concern' and warned that its financing was in jeopardy. Mr. Andrews said that the group appeared to advocate 'the acceptance and support for homosexuality as a lifestyle.'

In December, Mr. Andrews informed Ms. Walker that his board had decided to establish a separate United Methodist campus ministry and would be withdrawing its support of the Christian community.

Ms. Walker said that she still does not understand what Mr. Andrews objected to, and that the Campus Christian Community was following the same guidelines as the United Methodist Church. 'The Methodist [Book of] Discipline says that all people are of sacred worth, and we feel we are being true to that,' she said.

Pastor Burt, who is now associate dean of the chapel at Chicago, said she was disturbed to see the breakup of a long-standing partnership. 'The Campus Christian Community is a wonderful community that welcomes diversity and discussion and disagreement. And its very sad to me that it may be coming to an end,' she said.

A Changing Reputation

A statement by the Virginia Conference announcing the decision to form a new ministry at Mary Washington College made no mention of the issue of homosexuality. Instead, the change was attributed to a desire to further the outreach of higher-education ministries, and Mr. Andrews declined to comment on the controversy.

Members of the Campus Christian Community board wrote a letter in January asking the United Methodist board to reconsider its decision. Mr. Andrews said the board would discuss the request at its biannual meeting January 30. Alumni and students have also been urged to write letters. Board members were especially upset about the church's claim to the building because a recent addition was financed jointly by the four denominations.

Ironically, the Campus Christian Community has gained a reputation on campus for becoming less hospitable to gay men and lesbians since Pastor Burt's departure. Students have laid the blame on the interim pastor, Mochel Morris, a United Methodist. Last Spring, Ms. Morris removed the Reconciled in Christ certificate from a wall in the group's center. She also removed a basket of condoms and a supply of pamphlets written by Pastor Burt entitled 'Our Sexuality is a Gift from God.'

Ms. Morris, who declined to comment about the criticisms of her, told the campus newspaper in October that she made the changes because 'we do not feel that our primary mission is people's sexuality.' She said gay and lesbians students were still welcome to participate.

But some students disagree. 'There's really a difference in tolerating people who come, and embracing who they are,' said Ms. Neidig, a junior who is a member of both the Campus Christian Community and Pride Reflecting Individuals of Sexual Minorities. 'Sex as a whole is just kind of checked at the door, whereas before it wasn't taboo to talk about it.'

4. It's time to re-imagine our relationships

Written before the 2000 General Conference, this commentary suggests that we need to learn how to dialogue with our opponents. Perhaps this is true, but for some, dialogue with a racist, a homophobe, or a sexist is tantamount with dialogue with the devil.

United Methodist News Service, January 25, 2000
by the Rev. Robert W. Barnes*

In a few months, General Conference will convene and adjourn in Cleveland for either the first or the last time in the century, depending on how you count to a hundred. After a whirlwind of meetings and decisions, some of which we will actually understand, most United Methodists will be relieved that we have held together for another four years. The battles will be over, the votes taken, and probably not a lot will have changed.

Do you ever wish that we could do better?

All of us know that when the secular press reports on our General Conference, the headline story will be our quadrennial debate over homosexuality. Most of us are tired of fighting the same war over and over again, and it is tempting to believe that if this argument would miraculously disappear we would have unity.

This is wrong-headed. We United Methodists are not divided because of homosexuality. We are divided because we are divided. If there were no such thing as homosexuality, our divisions would be manifested in some other arena. Until we address these divisions, we will never 'do better.'

The funny thing is that our great weakness, our lack of theological unity, is also potentially the great strength of the United Methodist denomination. When the Wesleyan followers of Jesus have made the largest difference in the world it has been because as a movement we have blended a variety of Christian perspectives and passions, creating a church that is 'bright as the sun, fair as the moon and terrible as an army with banners.'

Our problem today is not that we have Christians who do not always think and act alike. Our problem today is that we have forgotten how to work together with those who are different.

It is overly simplistic to speak of 'conservatives and liberals.' Unfortunately, there is no better way to describe our theological identity crisis.

Methodists have always been blessed by the presence of both conservative and liberal Christians. By conservative Christians, I refer to men and women who are energized by the power and authority of God's word. Theirs is a vertical faith. Conservative Christianity calls men and women to repent of their sins and accept the salvation God has offered. It guards the truth, defends the word and proclaims the gospel.

Liberal Christians tend to be more horizontal. Their great commandment is to love their neighbors as themselves in a world where everyone is their neighbor. Liberal Christians reach out for the hurting and marginalized, doing everything in their power to feed the hungry, lift up the fallen and include the excluded. Their watchword is: 'Let justice roll down like a mighty river.'

These definitions need not suggest that conservative Christians are uncaring or that liberals never read their Bibles and pray. Most of us are far more balanced than that. The thing is, most Christians are either energized primarily by the conservative or the liberal impulse. We have theological orientations, if you will. Either nothing is so serious as the eternal word of God or so pressing as the latest great social cause. Our job in reconstructing the denomination has to be to find a way to blend what is right with conservatism and liberalism. If we don't, we will continue to war among ourselves, or worse yet, settle for a bland faith without conviction.

Let's be honest. We need each other. Without liberals, conservative Christians would find it too easy to walk around in their own little worlds of scholarship, biblical prophecy and church growth. I thank God for the liberals who come to us and say 'go.' Go to the hungry. Go to the homeless. Go to the excluded. Go to those who struggle in sin. I think Jesus wants conservatives to listen to these voices and has promised that not even the gates of hell will prevail against us when we do.

Conversely, liberals need conservatives because they know how to say 'no.' No to philosophical trends that take us away from the gospel. No to surrendering essentials of the Christian faith. No to losing our distinctive identities as Christians. If conservatives need liberals to tell them what to do, liberals need conservatives to remind them of who they are.

The time has come for us to re-imagine our relationships with one another, to see brothers and sisters in Christ where once we saw 'narrow minded bigots' and 'godless heretics.' (Isn't it always easier if our enemies are awful people?) To do this, we will have to repent of our theological prejudices and hardened hearts.

It will be hard. It will feel risky. The thing is, until we find unity, we will not be able to share the good news as a denomination, to homosexuals, or to anyone else for that matter.

Sometimes the hardest fight we face is the battle to make peace.

*Rev. Barnes is pastor of Bedington United Methodist Church in Martinsburg, W.Va. This column previously appeared in UM Connection, the newspaper of the Baltimore Washington Annual Conference.

Part IV OTHER CHURCHES AND SECULAR INSTITUTIONS SUPPORT US: COMING OUT FROM ISOLATION

Overcoming the Barriers of Loneliness and Fear

"I am the door of the sheep ... and I have other sheep"
(John 10:7, 16 RSV)

by Barbara

THE NARRATIVE

While we were working through our family trauma we were also learning about homosexuality and finding help from various sources. We were surrounded by many friends, some of whom were the age of our parents and served as surrogate family members for us. We spoke with various members of the clergy who had a reputation of being open minded and asked their advice about our situation. Virtually all said that we were on a long and possibly rough road to reconciliation. Some even intervened on our behalf by speaking to my parents with a word of interpretation and challenge. We were disappointed by our denomination's foot dragging, but found help from many supportive individuals and from many groups which had grown out of the church.

We were surprised when we learned about the experiences of a family we had known when we lived in New Concord. Jan and Taylor Stultz were prominent people in the community in which we had lived for eight years. Two of their three sons came out as homosexuals long after we had left the community. We had not been aware of this until a friend told us of a news program about the research into the causes of homosexuality. It was hosted by celebrated news analyst Roger Mudd and featured the Stultz family and others. The program gave tentative support to a genetic view of the cause of homosexuality. Not only did this program give us information about links between homosexuality and biology, it demonstrated that many families were struggling with the same challenges as we were. We were not alone!

We began to hear stories about other students whom we had known in earlier years, who since then had come out as homosexuals. We met other parents of homosexuals, and together we all grew. Both Reg and I sought some counseling. One psychiatrist said it was not really rational to expect that people the age of our parents would ever change their minds on such a topic. He urged that Reg turn his mind to other things.

In 1997 we attended a conference sponsored by various Lutheran groups—the Phillip N. Knutson Endowment, "Lutherans Concerned," and others at the University of Michigan. Its title was "The Gifts We Offer The Burdens We Bear." We heard various speakers, and attended panel discussions, workshops and worship services. Two statements from the conference program set the tone for the meeting. An anonymous minister said, "The great gift of being a gay pastor is the love that I receive from parishioners as I share with them both the desert places of their hurts and the oases of their joyful moments. The burden is, of course, the tortured irony that I am not able to share my secret lonely and joyful places as a gay man with them." One of the presenters, Lisa Lange, said, "When I realized that I was a lesbian, I stopped attending church because I was afraid that God didn't accept me. After numerous hours of prayer and study of the Bible I came to understand that God accepts me even if the church doesn't. I look forward to the day when I can feel welcome to participate in all aspects of church life while being honest about who I am."

We felt refreshed when we gathered to sing religious songs together, some of which had been appropriated by evangelicals who were so often homophobic. We sang, "Surely the presence of the Lord is in this place, I can feel his mighty power and his grace. I can hear the brush of angel's wings, I see glory on each face; Surely the presence of the Lord is in this place." We found God in the presence of these very spiritual and open persons! We also sang, "What does the Lord require of you? What does the Lord require of you? To seek justice, and love kindness, and walk humbly with your God." Yes, we thought, this is an issue of social and religious justice.

During this period of growth we read an article by Walter Wink, Professor of Biblical Interpretation at Auburn Theological Seminary in New York City, entitled "Homosexuality and the Bible," published in *Fellowship*, March/April, 1997 (12 15). This article gave an outline of inconsistencies in the biblical view of sexuality in general and homosexuality in particular.

Our education continued when we attended a "gay pride" march. Of course there were the flamboyant, and sometime vulgar representations which are so often targeted by the press, but we were amazed to see several floats sponsored by religious groups in support of gays and lesbians, often featuring biblical quotations! The same weekend of the gay pride march we attended the Hennepin Avenue United Methodist Church in Minneapolis, Minnesota. We were pleased to learn that this large and prestigious congregation was a Reconciling Congregation. This is a program sponsored by representatives of the United Methodist Church who urge churchmen and churchwomen to accept homosexuals. It was affirming to hear about the struggles this church had undertaken, including being picketed by a religious right wing hate group, the Westboro Baptist Church of Topeka, Kansas.

We were constantly challenged by the stories of others' painful experiences as homosexuals who had been victimized, even by the church! One prominent citizen had spent four days a week for six years in psychoanalysis with a homophobic Jewish psychoanalyst. He had received "help" from a variety of other counselors all who tried to help him go straight! Finally, he found a nonjudgmental Catholic psychiatrist. After working with this non-homophobic counselor the gay man said, "I have harbored deep and very self-destructive anger for most of my life." We thank God that this person survived the efforts of the homophobic "helping" professionals!

We heard the painful stories of gays and lesbians who experienced rejection when they came out to family, friends, and church people. We were somewhat amazed to learn that this pain and rejection was matched when religious homosexuals "came out" as Christians to members of the gay community. "Why would you expose yourself to condemnation by such self righteous religious people?" they are asked. It seems ironic, that many homophobic church-goers say that they "hate the sin" (of homosexuality), but can "love the sinner," (homosexuals). Unfortunately, many homosexuals do not feel loved, but feel personally rejected by the church! This is a matter which conservative church-goers must address.

We were invited to give devotions at a reunion of the families of graduate students who had been active in the North Broadway United Methodist Church in Columbus, Ohio. The group had been called "Betwixt and Between." We had not seen these friends for thirty years. As we all spent time reminiscing and bringing others up to date with our own life stories, we decided to include the story of our own pilgrimage relating to the "gay issue." As we poured out our hearts to these old friends we saw points of contact and sympathy from some, who, like us had been struggling with the issue, and we saw rejection and even latent hostility in the eyes of others who clearly were in opposition to homosexuality, and resented our dealing with the subject on this otherwise "happy" occasion. Well, what are reunions for? They are a time to learn what has been going on over the years. We would only hope that our next reunion will find more understanding people who have grown on the issue, partly due to our own personal witness on the subject.

Local groups of Reconciling United Methodists (RUMS) have been meeting across the country to support one another, invite congregations to consider inclusive statements, and gather resources to offer to congregations who accept the invitation. We have been involved in these gatherings and have appreciated the opportunity to share our story with others, and hear theirs in return.

In 1998 we attended a retreat in Michigan called "Building Bridges." It was a regional conference of the Reconciling Congregation Program. People from Michigan, Indiana, and Ohio gathered to hear nationally recognized speakers David Otto, Associate Professor of Religion at Centenary College, Shreveport, Louisiana; Theresa McClelland, staff reporter of the Grand Rapids Press; and two leaders of the Reconciling Congregation Program Mark Bowman and James Preston. This weekend retreat helped us experience the vitality of the Reconciling Congregation Program.

We helped to start a PFLAG chapter in our own town. Our "Parents, Family and Friends of Lesbians and Gays" is a support group which is a part of the national PFLAG network. This group also supported us in our continuing growth. The individuals to whom we grew close became like a second family to us. I became the president of our fledgling chapter. In our meetings we met many who were parents of homosexuals, many gay people themselves, and many more who were there just because they cared. These contacts were helpful in giving us insight and courage to face our trials of the moment, but they also gave us a sense of mission that would eventually lead to our pursuit of change in the Church itself! Altogether, these experiences helped us to come out from the isolation which forces some families of homosexuals to "hide in the closet" of loneliness and fear, even from the church!

We gave a prayer of gratitude that the Lord makes known God's will in so many ways, even outside the Church!

THE DOCUMENTS

1. Homosexuality, the subject the church does not want to examine

The words of Walter Wink made such an impression on Reg that he used Wink's arguments in an educational paper on Homosexuality and the Bible for students and others.

by Reg Olson, 1999

WHAT DOES THE BIBLE SAY ABOUT HOMOSEXUALITY?*

1. 'Homosexuality,' as a life style, a desire, and a self concept is a new notion, little more than 100 years old! So the Bible treats 'homosexuality' in the same manner as it treats the Internet, that is, it says NOTHING directly about it!

2. The Bible speaks of an incident in the city of Sodom, in Genesis 19:1-11, which many scholars say is a violation of the cultural conception of hospitality, not a condemnation of sodomy as a sexual act.[2] This story is most accurately seen as a rejection of violent gang rape, intended to humiliate others.

3. The Leviticus 18:22 and 20:13 admonitions against 'unnatural acts' are part of the holiness code, a list of acts which make one ritually impure. This code governed

the priesthood, as a prerequisite for their entering temple, and is generally not binding on Christians today.[3]

4. The Romans 1:24-27 reference to men and women who have 'unnatural relations' with same sex partners is given in the context of behaviors, indicative of an upheaval of society, which are the outcome of idolatry, not a list of sins in and of themselves.[4]

5. Nowhere does Jesus say anything about same sex behaviors.[5]

6. No injunction against same sex behaviors appears in the ten commandments.

7. Even if the Bible is talking about homosexual acts it condemns many other behaviors, including greed, gluttony, adultery, usury and drunkenness. Few church people today say that because of participation in any of these behaviors, the church ought not to marry a couple, or ordain a candidate for ministry!

WHAT DOES THE BIBLE SAY ABOUT THOSE WHO ARE EXCLUDED FROM MAINSTREAM SOCIETY?

It says that Jesus ate with sinners, and tax collectors, and took time to speak to a Samaritan Woman (in violation of social standards of his day). The Bible tells us that our purpose as Christians should be to be reconcilers. '...You are all baptized in Christ, you have all clothed yourselves in Christ, and there are no more distinctions between Jew and Greek, slave and free, male and female, but all of you are one in Christ Jesus." Galatians 3:26-28 (Does this logically exclude homosexuals?)[6]

WHAT DOES THE BIBLE SAY ABOUT SEX?

1. There are many areas of contemporary agreement with biblical sexual rules- for instance, rejection of incest,

rape, adultery, intercourse with animals.[7]

2. Many Christians today disagree with the Bible's condemnation of naming sexual organs, nudity,[8] birth control, celibacy and divorce,[9] and intercourse during menstruation.[10]

3. The Bible permitted behaviors which we condemn today: prostitution, polygamy and concubinage,[11] the levirate marriage,[12] sex with slaves,[13] and treatment of women as property.

4. Walter Wink concludes that 'the Bible has no sexual ethic. Instead, it exhibits a variety of sexual mores, some of which changed over the thousand-year span of biblical history.

WHAT DOES SCIENCE TELL US?

1. Science tells us that there is no necessary connection between four behaviors which we seem to equate with 'homosexuality.' These are pederasty (sexual attraction of older adults to children), homophilia (a same-sex attraction between adults), transvestism (cross-dressing), and sexual aggression and violence.

2. Over 400 animal species practice some form of homosexual relationships.

3. Many contemporary Christian churches do not condemn loving, responsible homosexual relationships. They accept, marry and ordain homosexuals. These include the Metropolitan Community Church; many Quaker, Unitarian Universalist churches, United Churches of Christ, and some Episcopal dioceses.[14]

WHAT DO CHURCH HISTORY AND SOCIOLOGY REVEAL TO US?

1. That homosexuals have been targeted by hate groups and have been victims of murder and gay bashing.[15]

2. That the church has a higher rate of homosexual participants than the general society at large.

3. That many homosexual participants in the church have played key leadership roles.[16]

4. That many homosexuals, with great talents and graces, would serve the church, but are denied ordination.

5. That the church has often condemned homosexuals, and that the church has often rejected certain populations, only to repent of this ostracism later (such as the division of the churches over slavery into separate denominations).

6. That many Christian homosexuals have been alienated from the church, and have left the fellowship.[17] What is the problem? While many church people wonder, 'why are people homosexual?,' others wonder, 'why are church members homphobic?'[18]

FOOTNOTES

* Biblical scholars are not in complete agreement in their interpretation of what the Bible says about homosexuality (or on many other subjects, for that matter). What follows is a set of rationales given by many church scholars for an alternative interpretation of key texts and issues.

1. Furnish says,'... the ancient world had no conception of either 'heterosexuality' or 'homosexuality' as distinct orientations.')Victor Paul Furnish, 'Understanding Homosexuality in the Bible's Cultural Particularity,' *The Circuit Rider*, Dec. 1991/January 1992, page 10.)

2. Indeed, Lot tells the townspeople they can 'have' his virgin daughters, which would hardly please a 'homosexual' man! Ezekiel 16:48-50 says that the real sin of the people of Sodom was their abundance of material goods, and their failure to meet the needs of the poor, and their worship of idols. He does not mention any sexual

behavior. In Luke 10:10-13 Jesus says that Sodom and Gomorrah will be treated more kindly than any city that mistreats and rejects his disciples. 'The connection between the mistreatment of Lot's guests and Jesus' disciples is quite clear.' From Presbyterian Church (USA), *Reports, the 203rd General Assembly* (1991), Part I (sexuality report). See also Judges 19: 22-30 for a parallel account of a gang rape of a concubine.

3. This same holiness code includes admonitions against eating animals declared unclean. It condemns wearing clothing of mixed fibers, eating shellfish, and eating rare meat. It also says that a man who is maimed, or deformed cannot be ordained as a priest. It seems especially concerned with various pagan practices (including cult prostitution), which compromised Israel's loyalty to God. These specific acts can be contrasted with the view of 'holiness' given by Isaiah, which emphasizes corporate and personal justice.

4. This is the only biblical statement with a possible reference to lesbian behavior. Paul seems especially concerned with the practices of male prostitution and pederasty. Furthermore, Paul is not describing a relationship between consenting adults in a committed relationship. Paul's main point seems to be that, 'all have sinned and fallen short of the glory of God,' Romans 3:22-23. Sin is living apart from God, not just committing a specific act from a list of forbidden behaviors.

5. Jesus' own lifestyle, in which he kept company with a band of men, whom he had taken away from their wives and families and trades, and preached a gospel of love, may have been seen as strange by many contemporary critics of same sex relationships, as would have been the relationship David had with Jonathan, which was said to 'exceed his love for women' (2 Samuel 1:26).

6. It suggests that slavery is part of God's good plan. It says that the Hebrews should slay the inhabitants of the land of Canaan (ethnic cleansing?) Some biblical injunctions are indeed culture bound, while others are of lasting significance, such as the declaration that God loves the poor. It condemns greed, saying that greedy people cannot get to heaven easily. It says that we are to love our neighbor as ourself. It says that God accepts sinners, as did the father of the Prodigal Son.

7. (From Walter Wink, of Auburn Theological Seminary) 'Homosexuality and the Bible' in *Fellowship* March/April, 1997.) Adultery was punishable by death (Deut. 22:22), and a bride found not to be a virgin was to be stoned (Deut. 22:13-21).

8. Nudity, even in one's home, was considered reprehensible, to the extent that spouses could not view each other unclothed at any time (2 Sam. 6:20; 10:4; Isaiah 20:2-4).

9. The Old Testament allows for divorce (Deut. 24:1-4), and sees celibacy as normal, while the New Testament forbids divorce (Mark 10:1-2) and calls compulsory celibacy a heresy (1 Tim. 4:1-3).

10. Failure to avoid women in menstruation was punishable by death (Lev. 18:29).

11. Polygamy and concubinage were regularly practiced in the Old Testament and never condemned there or in the New Testament.

12. The levirate was a practice where a childless widow was to have intercourse with each of her deceased husband's brothers in turn, until she bore a male heir. Jesus mentions this without any criticism in Mark 12:18-27.

13. The use of slaves as sexual toys or breeding machines or involuntary wives was explicitly permitted 2 Sam. 5:13, Judges 19-21, and Numbers 31:18.

14. See Bruce Bagemihl, *Biological Exuberance. St. Martin Press.*

15. Homosexuals were forced to wear pink triangles on their prison garb in Nazi camps, as the Jews wore yellow stars. Cargas notes that, "The most serious organized attack on same sex lovers in history was instituted by Hitler and his followers. ... The best scholarly estimates are that the number of gay men and women murdered solely because of their sexual orientation was between 5,000 and 20,000,' (Harry James Cargas, in *Fellowship*, December 1991, page 18). One wonders if the people who have committed violent acts against homosexuals, such as the murder of Matthew Shepard in Wyoming, were affected by the admonitions of churches against homosexuality.

16. 'There are substantial numbers of persons of homosexual orientation within the church whose gifts and graces manifest the work of the Spirit among us' (from the final report of the United Methodist Committee to Study Homosexuality, 1992).

17. While it is said to be very difficult for homosexual persons to 'come out of the closet' (and reveal their sexual orientation) in a Christian circle, it is even more difficult for gay persons to "come out Christian" (reveal their Christian identity) in homosexual circles. This is because the Church is seen, rightly or wrongly, as the enemy of homosexuals!

18. Homophobia refers to fear of, (and perhaps hatred of) homosexuals.

2. Brighton area chapter of PFLAG

We incorporated our local PFLAG chapter on May 21, 2001, with 28 Charter Members.

by Reg Olson, 2001

Dear Friends:

We are now PFLAG chapter! Officially we are 'PFLAG, Brighton Area Chapter.' We had two good organizational meetings on May 7, 2001 and May 21. We now have 30 paid members (dues are $15 per person, if you want to join).

The purposes for which the corporation is organized are:

a. to hold and manage property and funds for charitable purposes, including the assistance and support of charitable institutions, associations and undertakings;

b. to provide a support system for families and friends of lesbians and gays in their effort to understand, accept, and support their children with love and pride;

c. to provide education for individuals and the community at large on the nature of homosexuality;

d. to support the full human rights and civil rights of lesbians and gays; and

e. to speak out and act whenever necessary to defend and enhance those human rights and civil rights.

Our meeting topics for the summer are:

June 11 'Causes of Homosexuality,' with a PBS video.
July 9 'PFLAG's initiative for the public schools.'
August 13 'Being Gay in Brighton.'

Brighton PFLAG formed a coalition with twenty other organizations

Dear Members of the Safe Schools Coalition:

Thank you for joining us in coalition for this important project which focuses on making the social environment of the schools and community life free from harassment, bullying and intimidation of children regardless of their race, ethnic background, physical ability, physical stature, gender, sexual orientation, religion, mental capability, learning style and other differences.

The Brighton Community and Northern Schools will celebrate a day of diversity awareness and education on Monday April 22. Creating Safe Space in our schools and community will be considered and discussed by educators at an afternoon in service training seminar.

A Public Forum on Monday April 22 at 7 PM in the evening will offer parents and concerned citizens an opportunity for learning how feeling unsafe and insecure in our schools and community affects our children and students. A panel of persons will speak about the reality of bullying and intimidation and its negative results in the education process and social growth. Positive methods for addressing these issues and creating learning opportunities will be addressed.

Respect for the humanity of all persons is the goal of the coalition for 'Safe Schools in a Safe Community Day'. At their meeting on April 16, the Brighton City Council declared By Proclamation that April 22, 2002 will officially be 'Safe Schools in a Safe Community Day' in Brighton, Ohio.

3. Safe schools in a safe community project

One of Brighton PFLAG's projects was the Safe Schools project, a priority of the national PFLAG organization. In Brighton there were many public discussions of this topic, such as my speech at the Christian Center's Food for Thought Luncheon.

by Barbara Olson, October 31, 2002

Today I want to bring you a report on the Safe Schools in a Safe Community Project here in Brighton. In light of recent abusive events it might be said that this project is quite timely. (There was a cross burning in the yard of a multi-racial family, and harassing e-mail messages were received by students who signed an add for 'Coming Out Day' in the local newspaper.) Actually, since the project has been on the table for most of this year, it cannot be said that we are reacting specifically to these events but, these events surely point to the need for education and understanding in our town.

The Goal of the Safe Schools in a Safe Community Project here in Brighton is to enhance the quality of human interaction at all levels and for all people in our community. Safety and Security are at the root of achieving this quality.

Our Objectives are to provide education on diversity issues, on causes of abuse and on ways to create safer environments. Since most organizations in the Brighton Area share a concern about abusive behaviors that undermine our safety and security, it is very important that we develop Coalition Partners and seek ways for all to interact and work to achieve the goals of the project.

On April 22, 'Safe Schools in a Safe Community Day' was proclaimed by City Council. Twenty community groups, churches and organizations signed on as sponsors for the project. An in-service training was made possible for the teachers at the high school and the middle school, and an evening public forum was held.

On November 8-10, a workshop entitled FREEDOM FOR ALL FROM BULLYING AND HARASSMENT will be held in which the participating organizations will share their concerns for making Brighton a more welcoming and safe place. Special consideration will be given to support of schools and our children. We will learn methods of handling difficult situations, prepare ourselves to be speakers and resource persons in the community and learn how to relate to the organizations represented. I invite all of you to join us for the weekend workshop. There is no cost to you, just your time and interest. To register just give me your name and contact information. The schedule is listed on the agendas on your tables and all the sessions are being held at the LCNB Meeting Room.

How did this begin? A year and a half ago a PFLAG chapter was incorporated here in Brighton. The mission of PFLAG (Parents, Friends and Families of Lesbians and Gays) is "to promote the health and well-being of all GLBT persons, their families and friends, through support to cope with an adverse society, education to enlighten an ill-informed public and advocacy to end discrimination and secure equal civil rights for all. PFLAG provides an opportunity for dialogue about sexual orientation and gender identity and acts to create a society that is healthy and respectful of human diversity.

Soon after the local chapter began, with a strong core of 35 members, we became aware of a National PFLAG Program, 'From Our House to the Schoolhouse.' As we began to look at the program and talk with school leaders, it became apparent that such a project could be a catalyst for change in this community. It also became apparent that as closely entwined as our community, university and schools are, efforts should be directed to the whole by as many groups as are willing to participate. We realize that GLBT persons are not the only ones who are the subjects of taunts, harassment, bullying, intimidation and physical acts of violence. Therefore, it is important for the 'Safe Schools in a Safe Community Project' to create safe environments for all.

(As an aside I should note that GLBT epithets, such as "fag", "dyke", "gay", "queer", "homo", and "lesbian" are used in the harassment of many persons regardless of whether they are homosexual or not! Perhaps now that racial epithets are actually illegal, using the unprotected Gay terms to harass anyone seems acceptable!)

Grant proposals were solicited by PFLAG National and the Gill Foundation from chapters that were actively involved in implementing programs on Creating Safe Schools and Affecting Change in Public Policy. The Brighton Chapter responded with grant applications to both programs and was successful in receiving grants from both *in an amount greater than that given to any other chapter* in the country, $5,000.00. This money was allotted for the Community Events in April; for providing educational materials to university, school and community persons and organizations; and for the presentation of the Workshop on November 8-10.

For all the coalition building efforts, programming and planning the Brighton Chapter received a National Award for Advocacy at the National PFLAG Conference in September.

We welcome participation of many Brighton organizations and churches. So much more can be accomplished with the synergy of many working together. Others who have not joined are welcome and encouraged to participate in the upcoming workshop. Again, if you are interested please speak to Reg or me.

Why are the Olsons so involved and continuing to be a presence even though we now live a distance away? Most of you know that our eldest daughter is a Lesbian. Many of you are aware of her and our story. If not, we will gladly share. However, it is important to note that our greatest parental concern for her and her life partner is their safety. We worry when they are traveling into unknown environments. Unfortunately, they have found churches to be among the least welcoming places to be. Fortunately, they have found welcoming congregations that do make a difference, but they are still few and far between.

These women are professionals. One is seminary trained and seeking to be a minister. Both have had major responsibilities such as Youth Congress officer, Church-related college student leadership and U-2 missionary. Yet the Methodist Church has disallowed Ordination and we feel it has turned its back on the baptism vows made by congregations when they were infants.

We are concerned that Gays are belittled for the way in which they were created by God. We are concerned for all the wonderful experiences being missed in our society by excluding talented people, whatever their difference. We are not an inclusive society in either secular or religious contexts. Some areas do better than others and we all have much to learn and practices to change.

Regardless of your views on homosexuality (we realize that there are many different views) we hope that you are concerned enough about the Safe Schools in a Safe Community Project here in Brighton.

4. Bishop Jack Tuell calls for PFLAG alliance

Here is an e-mail from a PFLAG leader along with one from a bishop. It was good to hear that the bishop said kind things about Parents, Family and Friends of Lesbians and Gays.

by Paul Beeman, Wednesday, 17 May 2000

Friends -

I just received the following letter from United Methodist Bishop Jack M. Tuell. He moved away from his mildly anti-gay position, unfavorable to homosexuality in The United Methodist Church, after presiding at the trial of The Rev. Gregory Dell last year for officiating at a holy union. He now advocates strongly for full rights for gays in the denomination and was a powerful influence at the recently concluded General Conference.

He noted to me that the anti-gay votes had diminished most in 1996, at which time the right wing of the church took up arms to stop their losses. The votes were as follows on motions of non-concurrence regarding change: 1988, 80.8%; 1992, 74.9%; 1996, 60.4%; 2000, 60.6% not to remove the 'incompatible' language, and 60.9% to turn down a minority report admitting differences of opinion on gay issues. It seems we did not lose as badly as some of us thought.

Please circulate this as you may feel appropriate. His letter follows.

With thanks, Paul Beeman, PFLAG national president.

Jack M. Tuell, Bishop,
The United Methodist Church, Retired May 18, 2000

Rev. Paul Beeman, President, PFLAG
Dear Paul,

Just a note to express profound thanks for your presence and the presence of so many PFLAG folks at [The United Methodist General Conference in] Cleveland. I believe they are the most effective proponents for change in our U[nited] M[ethodist] position. They carried great impact. As we look to the future, I hope it might be possible for PFLAG folks who are U[nited] M[ethodist]s to come together in some grouping as we look toward [our next General Conference in] 2004, to join with others in advocating for change. I think it important to have a group of only U[nited] M[ethodist]s, to avoid the 'carpetbagger' label. I even have a name [to suggest]: 'The Whole Gospel Movement.' The cause is by no means lost. Twelve years ago in 1988, the vote against change [in the official statement, 'homosexuality is incompatible with Christian teaching'] was 80.8%. This year it was 60.6%. The tide of knowledge and understanding may be moving slowly, but it is moving!

Sincerely,
Jack M. Tuell, Bishop,
The United Methodist Church

5. The Grand Rapids PFLAG Regional Meeting

As we got more involved in PFLAG we were invited to

attend a regional meeting.

by Reg Olson, October, 2001

The October, 2001 Regional PFLAG meeting was held in Grand Rapids, Michigan. The hotel in which the meeting was held was a nice location for the meeting, as the staff was very cooperative. For the first part of the meeting PFLAG occupied a whole wing of the convention center. On the last day of the meeting, however, the facilities were shared with a wedding reception. This proved to be interesting when the large hallway in which the PFLAG exhibits were displayed was divided in half with a small barrier.

There was little contact between the two groups, although there were some 'long looks' at the PFLAG exhibits, especially a large sign displayed by Ford Motors in support of employee diversity. Ironically, at one point, a couple of elderly wedding guests who did not want to push through the reception crowd to their Open Bar at the other end of the hall, stepped across the barrier and *bought drinks at the PFLAG cash bar!* Then they returned to their spouses on the other side. Was this a conscious step across a larger social barrier? Probably just the quenching of a thirst.

"Blessed are they who hunger and thirst
after righteousness."

Part V THE SOCIETY COMING OUT FROM HOMOPHOBIA AND HATE CRIMES
Overcoming the Barrier of Social Stigma

"The Lord will pass over the door . . ."
Exodus 12:23c

by Reg

THE NARRATIVE

The struggle to win acceptance and equal rights for persons regardless of their sexual identity is being fought on many fronts—in the classroom, the boardroom, the media, in local churches, in groups of concerned church people, and in denominational conferences. One wonders, given the level of acceptance of homosexuals in the society at large, if the struggles in the church are not anachronistic. Has the Church fallen behind the society on this social justice issue, instead of leading it? Many have seen the church as having properly played a leading role in the achievement of civil rights, women's rights, and the ending of the war in Vietnam. But, on the issue of homosexuality, as well as some others, the church seems to have given up its prophetic stance.

Homophobia has many faces. One is discrimination. Another is rejection. And then there is violence which is committed against gays. We have heard about Matthew Shepard, the story of a gay man who was tied to a fence, pistol whipped, and murdered. The testimony of Matthew Shepherd's parents at the murder trial was very poignant. Parents of gays and lesbians are naturally concerned about their well-being. Then there is the story of the Arthur J.R. Warren murder. He was a young man who was kicked to death because he was gay. After killing him, his assailants drove a car over his body several times to make the crime appear to be an auto accident. Crimes such as this have caused many people to propose that hate crimes legislation include protection of gays and lesbians. A hate crime is a crime directed against the whole class of people based on their race, ethnicity, gender, or sexual orientation. A hate crime is different from an assault or murder, in that it sends a message to *all the members of that class* of persons that they are in jeopardy. It is not the case that these crimes are just based on the bad feelings of the perpetrator but they are *aimed* to terrorize all the members of the victim's class. Unfortunately, many people today, especially church people, oppose the inclusion of sexual orientation in hate crimes legislation. This is because they believe that the hate crime legislation will give special privilege to homosexuals whom they believe deserve no special privileges. Furthermore, bias incidents are related to hate crimes in that they support a social climate of hatred against a group of persons. This hatred can be translated into acts of crime. It is not the case that hate alone is a punishable offense, but, that it can result in an act of violence. In the absence of *national* legislation aimed at hate crimes against a person's sexual orientation, localities and states are the major sources of current protections. Unfortunately, such hate crime legislation varies considerably from place to place. Furthermore, the reporting of such crimes is very uneven, as many victims are afraid to make a report for fear of retaliation against themselves by the very persons who allegedly committed the crimes.

Not only is there a lack of adequate reporting, the data-gathering itself is inadequate. And so we are left with a void in our knowledge of the extent to which these crimes are being perpetrated.

In Brighton, Ohio there have not been any more hate crimes than in any other community of its size, but there has been an awareness of the need for more adequate reporting and data gathering. For this reason the Community Relations Commission of which I have been a member, has sought to galvanize community action to clarify these issues relating to hate crimes. Public meetings have been called and committees have been set up, to make suggestions as to how to handle bias incidents and hate crimes.

Those who say that this concern about hate crimes sounds extreme need to go back to the history of the Nazi Holocaust to see how hate crimes came to define and shape a society's priorities. Millions of Jews, Gypsies, Jehovah Witnesses, ministers, and homosexuals were systematically weeded out and murdered.

So we are talking about a society-wide dilemma. How shall the nation deal with persons defined as deviants? In America many religious communities have defined homosexuals to be deviants beyond the pale. Southern Baptists have been especially vociferous in their opposition to homosexuals. Protestant evangelicals and members of other faith communities have likewise intimidated gays and lesbians. An example of this opposition is the "wisdom" of Dr. Laura Schlessinger, a radio commentator who has a doctorate in English, but lays claim to the authority of a religious leader. She has often pontificated about all sorts of moral dilemmas. Many people have taken Dr. Laura to task in a somewhat humorous fashion and have focused on the inconsistencies of her biblical interpretations. The issue is not that a commentator, clergy person or a church just takes a moral stance against something, but that it establishes a *climate* which breeds hatred and violence against the class of people.

This not only occurs among would-be experts and the clergy, but also occurs in voluntary associations such as the Boy Scouts of America. In that organization homophobia has emerged to the point where intolerance and discrimination against gay members has reached a fevered pitch. They have banned gay scout leaders, and, as a result, they have been taken to court for discrimination. On June 28, 2000, the United States Supreme Court held that the Scouts had a first amendment right to expel a highly decorated scoutmaster, as his presence would interfere with the Boy Scouts' right to express its anti-gay message. Ironically, this case, and other similar ones, has actually hurt the Scouts, as several corporate sponsors and United Way Agencies have withdrawn their support of the Boy Scouts of America.

There are also signs of reconciliation in our society. For instance, the Reform Jews have made statements in favor of the ordination of gay clergy. We have also seen countless corporations and businesses extending legal rights and privileges to gay couples in their midst. There is even a growing acceptance of homosexuality in many television shows. Many stereotypes still abound, but many myths are also being shattered. The Brethren/Mennonite Council for Lesbian and Gay Concerns recently published materials dealing with biblical references, and they put homophobia squarely in the context of human oppression. Another sign of social change is that Civil Unions have recently been legalized in the state of Vermont.

With the progress of the genome project, the mapping out of genetic data, we may be on the verge of a clearer understanding of the biological bases of homosexuality. One might expect that such information would put to rest the notion that homosexuals have chosen their lifestyle. But, unfortunately, many moralistic religious leaders have already gone on record saying that even if there is a genetic propensity toward homosexuality this would not excuse homosexual behaviors.

Whether our society becomes more tolerant of homosexuals will depend, in the long run, on the ability of the religious communities to be reconciled to gays and lesbians. Perhaps this reconciliation will not occur until the real reason why religious people oppose homosexuality has been exposed. I am convinced that the reason why so many religious people oppose homosexuality is because it undercuts male dominance in a society where the male prerogatives have already been strained and challenged. It is difficult for men to accept their vulnerability, but religion should not be used to maintain a social structure which routinely subordinates one group to another.

We pray that society would become more tolerant of homosexuality, and that homosexuals would be spared from any acts of violence and hatred which others might perpetrate against them.

THE DOCUMENTS

1. Hate crimes and bias incidents

The Brighton City Community Relations Commission, of which I was a member, started a task force on hate crimes. When I was asked to give a challenge to the task force I gave a speech at a community meeting. Later that year I gave an update on the speech at the Christian Center.

by Reg, 2000

A Talk at the Christian Center, Food for Thought Luncheon

In 1945 Rev. Martin Niemoller wrote these famous words:

'First they came for the Communists,
and I didn't speak up,
because I wasn't a Communist.
Then they came for the Jews
and I didn't speak up,
because I wasn't a Jew

Then they came for the Catholics
and I didn't speak up,
because I was a Protestant
Then they came for me,
and by that time there was no one
left to speak up for me'

In Brighton, Ohio there probably have not been any more hate crimes than in any other community of its size, but there is an awareness of the need for more adequate data and data reporting and gathering. For this reason the City of Brighton's *Community Relations Commission* of which I have been a member, was asked to galvanize community action to clarify these issues relating to hate crimes. I was asked to give an address at the November 30, 2000 Community Relations Commission's open forum. These are some of the comments I shared at that meeting.

I want to talk to you about Hate Crime Incidents ... On July 7, 1998 three white men dragged a black man, James Byrd, Jr. from the back of their pick up truck for three miles until parts of his body littered the roadside in Jasper, Texas. After Byrd's burial the Imperial Wizard of the KKK placed a KKK sticker on Byrd's grave stone ....

On April 20, 1999, Hitler's birthday, Isaiah Shoels, age 18, was shot in the head because he was black, and an athlete. Twelve others were also murdered at the Columbine High School, in Littleton, Colorado.

On October 12, 1998 Matthew Shepard, a homosexual man, was tied to a fence, and pistol whipped with a .357 Magnum and beaten so badly that he died shortly thereafter in Laramie, Wyoming. Some protested this act being called a hate crime and they attempted to use the 'gay panic' defense, saying that Shepard had made sexual advances. (This was denied in private testimony.)

On July 4, 2000 twenty-six year old Arthur Carl 'JR' Warren Jr., a gay African American man with mental and physical disabilities, was murdered in Grant Town, (population 400) West Virginia, by two 17 year olds and a 16 year old. The youths beat and kicked him with steel toed boots, and then ran him over twice with a car to disguise his death as a 'hit and run' accident. A human rights campaign worker said, 'There was incredible brutality in the beating... that kind of level of viciousness is what we often see in hate crimes.'

West Virginia had recently voted against expanding the state's hate crime law to include gays. A candle-light vigil took place at the Fairmont courthouse to ask why authorities were not considering this as a hate crime. The Rev. Fred Phelps, of the Topeka Kansas anti-gay group the Westboro Baptist Church picketed the vigil. He had also picketed the funeral of Matthew Shepard.

Private First Class Barry Winchell, a gay soldier was bludgeoned to death with a baseball bat while he slept, in his barracks in Fort Campbell, Kentucky in July, 1999.

Brighton knows about hate crimes. ... On Jan. 19, 1998, Jason Kindinger, an African American man was beaten by two youths with an axe handle on East Vine Street in Brighton, during which time the assailants made homophobic and racial slurs. There have also been sexual assaults against women and men in Brighton, and other hate crimes and bias incidents against people of color, international people and gays in our town.

People call these hate crimes. Some are very dramatic, indeed tragic, such as these examples, but thousands more never make it into the front page of the newspaper, or anywhere in the newspaper.

Hate crimes are defined as 'violent acts against people, property, or organizations because of the group to which they belong or are identified with' (race, religion, ethnicity, national origin, sexual orientation, disability or gender.) Hate crimes are 'message crimes.' They send a message to members of a certain group that they are unwelcome in a particular neighborhood, church, community, school, or workplace. The crime is against their very identity, their ancestry, or their families. 'Bias incidents' are different, in that no crime has been committed, although intimidation has occurred. It can be argued that in an environment where many bias incidents occur, the climate is ripe for hate crimes!

Opponents of the Hate Crimes Prevention Act note the difficulty of identifying an incident as being provoked by bias or hatred. One critic says that this all 'assumes that crimes are more or less serious depending on the thoughts and feelings of those who commit them.' He says facetiously, 'why not simply make hate illegal and penalize those who show any evidence of it?' We could legislate against George Orwell's *Thoughtcrime!*

We heard similar complaints during the Civil Rights movement of the 1960's. They said, 'You can't legislate morality" and, "You can't eliminate prejudice by religious conversion, or legislation.' But you **can** restrict people's opportunities to discriminate, to ACT or BEHAVE violently on the basis of their prejudices in a way which not only injures another person, but a WHOLE CLASS of persons.

Some people were so uncomfortable with the application of hate crimes laws to homosexuals that the state of Colorado passed an amendment banning laws that protect homosexuals from discrimination. When, in May 1996, the US Supreme Court struck that amendment down (in other words they said homosexuals *could be* protected) many objected. Will Perkins, author of the amendment and head of Colorado for Family Values, denounced the ruling. Lance Woodall, the CEO of Concerned Women for America, said that homosexuals should not have special protected status under the law. Phil Burgess, president of the Cincinnati based Citizens for Community Values, said if the judges have given sexual behavior a special-class status, that means that all other behaviors must be considered too. ...Smokers would have to be considered a minority class ... tall people, short people, and left handed people.

I find it intriguing that homophobic people would use the argument that homosexuals do not deserve "special rights" before the law. Special rights are not the problem, it is 'special wrongs' otherwise known as hate crimes, which have been targeting homosexuals, racial minorities, women, those with disabilities and others, special *wrongs* are the problem!

However, the arguments against hate crime legislative protection of gays have been made so effectively, that on October 13, 1998 the US Supreme Court allowed Cincinnati to ban laws that protect gay people from discrimination. It seems that gay people can't have special rights, but they can experience special wrongs.

Unfortunately, we don't really know very much about hate crimes due to a lack of adequate statistical evidence about them. Not until early 1990's did the federal government begin collecting data on how many and what kind of hate crimes are being committed, and by whom. Before 1991, when the Hate Crimes Statistics Act was passed, hate crimes were grouped together with homicide, assault, rape, robbery and arson. There are many differences in the ways states define and report this data. Seven states have no criminal penalties for hate crimes. Currently twenty-three states include sexual orientation in their hate crimes legislation. In 1996 law enforcement agencies in forty-nine states and Washington DC reported 8,769 bias-motivated offences to FBI. But data collected by the Anti-Defamation League, the National Asian Pacific American Legal Consortium, and the National Gay and Lesbian Task Force show a much higher incidence of hate crimes.

The statistics which have been kept show very uneven reporting. In 1996 only sixteen percent of law enforcement agencies reported ANY hate crimes in their regions. This means that eighty-four percent of the participating jurisdictions--including states with well documented histories of racial prejudice--reported NO hate crimes! If all reported hate crimes at the same rate we might expect 40,000 hate crimes to be recorded every year.

The data we do have shows that thirty percent of hate crimes in 1996 were crimes against **property**— robbing, vandalizing, destroying, stealing, or setting fire to vehicles, homes, stores, or places of worship. Seventy percent were attacks against **a person**— ranging from simple assault (no weapons involved) to aggravated assault, rape, murder. This is an attack on a person's body and also on one's identity. The Southern Poverty Law Center says college campuses rank as the third most common venue for hate crimes. ...

Before the FBI can classify an act as a hate crime they must answer the following questions:

a. Is the motive of the perpetrator known to be bias?

b. Does the victim perceive bias?

c. Are there any other reasons for the incident? (insanity, robbery, self defense)

d. Did the incident occur on or near a religious holiday?

e. Are there relevant demographic factors that might create resentment or bias? (age race, gender, ethnicity)

f. Are there any symbols involved in the incident that are associated with hate groups (such as Nazi swastikas)?

One reason why the data on hate crimes is so sketchy is because of the reluctance of victims to report attacks, out of fear of retaliation. Many victims also fear that the criminal justice system is biased against one's group. Hispanics and African Americans often express mistrust of the police.

Let's look at some of the trends in hate crime and bias incidents. Racial hatred is the largest category, making up forty percent of all hate crimes. [This includes violence against African Americans; some violence against white people; and historical violence against Asian Pacific Americans and Jews; harassment against Muslims and people of Arabic background.] ...

Did you know that 7.2 of every thousand women each year are rape victims? Perhaps rape has best been explained not as a 'crime of passion' as it is often portrayed in the media, but as an attempt to humiliate women and degrade them ...

Only in 1997 did America start collecting data on crimes against the disabled. It appears that the victims were seen as not equal, not deserving, not contributing members of society.

Anti-Gay Violence is the most socially acceptable and widespread form of hate crime among teens and young adults. Dr. Karen Franklin, fellow at the Washington Institute for Mental Illness Research and Training reports four types of assaulters against gays:

a. Ideology assailants— who see their violence as an enforcement of community morals,

b. Thrill seekers— who are making an attempt to feel strong,

c. Peer dynamics assailants— who would prove their toughness to heterosexual friends,

d. Self defense assailants— who believe homosexuals are sexual predators.

It is bad enough that so many have been murdered in hate crimes. But what of those who *survive* beatings, robberies, and vandalism? Psychologists tell us that victims of non-bias crimes typically take two years to overcome the stress of being victimized. In contrast, psychologists tell us, that victims of hate crimes may take as many as five years to overcome the ordeal of post traumatic stress disorder.

Proponents of the Hate Crimes Prevention Act of 1998 said the act would enlarge federal jurisdiction— expanding categories covered to include gender, sexual orientation and disability, and to allow federal investigations of all possible hate crimes. It did not pass in 1998, or 1999. When, in 2000 the newly named 'Local Law Enforcement Enhancement Act of 2000' passed the Senate (S622 by vote of 57) and passed the House of Representatives (HR 1082), by a vote of 232 to 192, on October 18, 2000 the American Family Association issued an 'action alert' to stop this act. They said that every crime they cover is already illegal, that they de-sensitize society to fighting crime in general, and that they are sponsored by homosexual activists. This legislation has not yet been enacted into law.

Why do people commit hate crimes? In general it is not due to organized hate groups. A study of hate crimes in Los Angeles in 1994-1995 discovered that fewer than five percent of the offenders were members of organized hate groups (i.e. neo-Nazis or 'skinheads'), but these are often the most dramatic. ...

Most offenders are otherwise law-abiding young people. The main determinant is personal prejudice, which blinds aggressors to the immorality of their acts. Offenders perceive that society sanctions attacks on certain groups. Dr. Karen Franklin, fellow at Washington Institute for Mental Illness Research and Training, has found, for instance, that in some settings there was a sense of **permission** for violence against homosexuals.

Consider for a moment, the story of Eric Rudolph who bombed an abortion clinic in Birmingham, Alabama, killing an off-duty policeman and maiming a nurse-on Jan uary 29, 1998. He seemed to believe that attempting to destroy a clinic that performs abortions is justified. It has been said that citizens of his home town, Andrews, North Carolina, have made him into a folk hero. They would normally say that blowing up somebody else's building is wrong, that killing someone while doing it is murder— but they have decided Rudolph's actions are justified. He is also charged in connection with the four fatal bombings at Olympic Park and elsewhere in Atlanta in which 150 people were injured. The FBI offered a $1,000,000 reward for him.

What can be done? Many positive things can be done. Social pressures and definitions of groups as 'sub-human,' or 'demonic,' undoubtedly contribute to the incidence of hate crimes. We prefer to blame hate crimes on organized hate groups and ignore the fact that in many ways *our society breeds hatred.* Our history of slavery, discriminating immigration laws, and differential gender power relations has an impact. Hate crimes are not necessarily random, or uncontrollable. Society can intervene to reduce or prevent violence among young people that threatens and intimidates entire categories of people.

We can support federal anti-discrimination laws, use the Community Relations Service (part of the Department of Justice) to resolve conflicts, support the training of police and victim-assistance professionals for early intervention techniques for hate crime victims, and educate to dispel minority stereotypes.

In Brighton public meetings have been called and committees have been set up, to make suggestions as to how to handle bias incidents as well as hate crimes. To date four study groups have been initiated: Reporting and Gathering Statistics of Hate Crimes, Victim Support Networks, Public Education About Hate Crime Trends, and Networking to Build Community Agreements About Dealing With Hate Crimes. Let us support their work.

Are victims of hate crimes people who have been given 'special treatment,' special rights, or are they victims of special wrongs?

2. Homosexuals and the Holocaust

It has been said that those who do not know their history may be doomed to repeat it. Let us become better informed about one of the groups victimized by the Third Reich.

From Ben S. Austin *An Introduction to the Holocaust*
The holocaust\shoah Internet page, August 10, 2000

THE NAZIS AND HOMOSEXUALS

During one of Hitler's purges in 1934 Ernst Roehm, a homosexual who was a leader of the SA (storm troopers) was murdered. The excuse that was given was the homosexuality of Roehm. Shortly thereafter Hitler ordered registration of all homosexuals and got the Reichstag to pass many laws against homosexuality. Those who were convicted under these laws had to wear pink triangles. In 1936 an office for Combating Homosexuality and Abortion was created. Those convicted of sex crimes were sent to concentration camps after serving their court-appointed prison sentence. Himmler suggested that homosexuality created a serious imbalance in the sex ratio, and constituted a threat to national security. A system of informants was created to gather anyone suspected of homosexuality. Attempts were made to educate or 'cure' homosexuality by 'medical' means. It is estimated that 10 to 15,000 homosexuals were exterminated in the concentration camps. In the camps those who wore the pink triangle were treated brutally by guards and other inmates. Most were exterminated within the first months of the camp experience. After the war homosexuality remained illegal until 1969 in Germany.

3. When were you supposed to start hating my son?

Perhaps no one can understand the rejection of a homosexual better than a parent. This does not mean

that all parents have this empathy and understanding, but some do, as the following powerful statement indicates.

By G. Mater, In Pflagcd.tripon.com

When were you supposed to start hating my son?

Was it when this beautiful baby boy was baptized before you and you promised to surround him in steadfast love and establish him in the faith? He was that same child at that moment that he is today.

Was it when you laughed at the clowning antics of this eager toddler with happy eyes and a smile that lit up his face?

Was it when you realized that this four year old was actually reading the books you passed out at 'looking' time?

Was it when you counted on him to eagerly participate in your classroom and help other students?

Was it when you handed him a Citizenship Award at the school assembly?

Was it when you gave him a top award in state competition?

Was it when you laid your hands on him during Confirmation?

Was it when you confided how you appreciated the loyal friendship he had given your child?

Was it when you selected him to receive the 'Spirit' award for his dedication to theater?

Was it when you chose him as 'outstanding club member' of the year?

Was it when you admired him for achieving the rank of Eagle Scout?

Was it when you told me that he is a true gentleman, even when no one is watching?

Was it when you congratulated him on earning scholarships for college?

I watched for clues to his interests and the natural directions in which he would grow. I encouraged, enriched and supported those inclinations. I wanted him to develop his full potential and blossom into the person God created him to be. He is the child that was born to be.

When was I supposed to start hating my son? Was it when I was grateful that he and his sister were so compatible. I dared to hope that they would become lifelong friends.

Was it when I noticed how carefully he handled books and toys? It was a sign of his intelligence. I wondered.

Was it when he recoiled, almost in horror, from being pulled into a romp on the floor with a visiting uncle and cousin? They were strangers. I wondered.

Was it when I saw how freely and naturally he moved to music? He really should have dance lessons. I decided not.

Was it when I marveled at the complex, imaginative structures that he built from anything blocks, sand, Legos, boxes, branches? He descends from engineers and woodworkers. I rejoiced.

Was it when I saw the tenderness and care he gave to plants and living creatures of all kinds? His ancestors were farmers. I was happy. And, I wondered.

Was it when the boys on the playground wouldn't allow him to take part in their recess games? He wept in anguish, 'I feel like they have taken my heart and wadded it up into a little ball and stomped on it.' I was devastated. And, I wondered.

Was it when I read his poetry or heard how eloquently he was able to put his feelings into words? Writing is a family gift. I was thrilled.

Was it when I listened to his music or saw his art or his love of opera? Artists and musicians are his heritage. I was proud. And, I wondered.

Was it when he could be moved to tears by sentimental losses - dinnerware replaced, wallpaper papered over, toys worn out? Many persons are sentimental. I wondered.

Was it when I found one of Grandpa's anatomy art books in his closet - the only one with both men and women nudes standing, stopping, sitting, walking, running, leaping? His curiosity was gratifying. But I wondered.

Was it when he didn't turn into a rebellious teenager suffering one crush after another? 'The Joy of Sex' was under his bed. I was glad that he was interested. And, I wondered.

Was I supposed to wonder when he was at the church each week - taking part in choirs, attending Sunday School, leading youth groups, serving on committees? I didn't. I was pleased.

When could I ever hate my son?

When did my son start deserving your hate?

He is the same child that he was yesterday and has been for all of the yesterdays since his birth. He has not changed. He has not been pretending, hiding or deceiving.

Today he discovered that God had given him a gift that he didn't expect. One that he did not understand earlier. One that he did not ask for or even want. It is a gift that he accepts because it is God-given.

Today he starts on his journey to manhood. He takes with him his love for his family, his church, his country, the earth and all of creation.

He dreams the same dreams as yesterday - getting an education, finding a job, having a home, volunteering in his church and community.

He dreams of being respected and of using his talents to do what he can to make our country and this world a little better place for everyone.

One day, he hopes to find the same personal

fulfillment, support and lasting commitment that every human being seeks and needs. He dreams of finding a man who will love him for himself - just as God created him.

When did you start hating my son? God blessed me. His providence provided that I would wonder, just enough, throughout my son's growing years that I can be open to the possibilities of his birthright.

I am filled with love, admiration, pride and hope for my son. Today my joy is subdued, because I am frightened. I do not fear my son or the many others amongst us.

I am afraid of you, And of what you may do to my son tomorrow. And, I am afraid for you.

4. Dr. Laura, June 2, 2000

Homophobia is not funny, but sometimes humor helps us to see truth. This message circulated on the Internet.

Original source unknown

BIBLICAL "TRUTH" FROM DR. LAURA

Dear Dr. Laura,

Thank you for doing so much to educate people regarding God's Law. I have learned a great deal from you, and I try to share that knowledge with as many people as I can. When someone tries to defend the homosexual lifestyle, for example, I simply remind him that Leviticus 18:22 clearly states it to be an abomination. End of debate. I do need some advice from you, however, regarding some of the specific laws and how to best follow them.

a. When I burn a bull on the altar as a sacrifice, I know it creates a pleasing odor for the Lord (Lev. 1:9). The problem is my neighbors. They claim the odor is not pleasing to them. How should I deal with this?

b. I would like to sell my daughter into slavery, as it suggests in Exodus 21:7. In this day and age, what do you think would be a fair price for her?

c. I know that I am allowed no contact with a woman while she is in her period of menstrual uncleanliness (Lev. 15:19-24). The problem is, how do I tell? I have tried asking, but most women take offense.

d. Lev. 25:44 states that I may buy slaves from the nations that are around us. A friend of mine claims that this applies to Mexicans, but not Canadians. Can you clarify?

e. I have a neighbor who insists on working on the Sabbath. Exodus 35:2 clearly states he should be put to death. Am I morally obligated to kill him myself?

f. A friend of mine feels that even though eating shellfish is an Abomination (Lev. 10:10), it is a lesser abomination than homosexuality. I don't agree. Can you settle this?

g. Lev. 20:20 states that I may not approach the altar of God if I have a defect in my sight. I have to admit that I wear reading glasses. Does my vision have to be 20/20, or is there some wiggle room here?

I know you have studied these things extensively, so I am confident you can help. Thank you again for reminding us that God's word is eternal and unchanging.

"Jeffrey"

5. Reform Jewish leaders approve same sex unions
It is refreshing when religious leaders move ahead to make a God-inspired witness. **GREENSBORO, N.C.**

The Associated Press, March 30, 2000

REFORM JEWISH LEADERS APPROVE SAME-SEX UNIONS

Reform Jewish leaders on Wednesday overwhelmingly approved a resolution giving rabbis the option of presiding at gay commitment ceremonies. With the vote, the Central Conference of American Rabbis became the most influential U.S. religious group to sanction same sex unions. The resolution applies to the 1,800 members of the Central Conference of American Rabbis, who serve at least 1.5 million Reform Jews. Reform Judaism is the largest and most liberal of Judaism's three major branches in North America, Rabbi Charles Kroloff, CCAR's president, said the resolution shows the conference's belief that 'gay and lesbian Jews, and the committed relationships they form with their partners, deserve the recognition and respect due to people created in the image of God.'

6. Civil Unions in Vermont!

In the year 2000 civil unions were legalized in the state of Vermont.

From American Anglican Council, web page,
Americananglican.org June 1, 2000

The Vermont Court Case (Baker v. Vermont)

Vermont has become the first state in which same-sex marriage has attained a toehold in the law. Three same-sex couples sued the State of Vermont in July of 1997 when they applied for marriage licenses and were denied. The case moved quickly to the Supreme Court, where numerous friend-of-the-court briefs were filed on both sides, including one brief in favor of same-sex 'marriage' supported by Episcopal clergy in Vermont.

On December 20, 1999, the Court issued a unanimous 5-0 decision reversing the decision of a lower trial court. The main opinion, written by three justices, stated:

> We hold that the State is constitutionally required to extend to same sex couples the common benefits and protections that flow from marriage under Vermont law. Whether this ultimately takes the form of inclusion within the marriage laws themselves or a parallel 'domestic partnership' system or some equivalent statutory alternative, rests with the Legislature. Whatever system is chosen, however, must conform with the constitutional imperative to afford all Vermonters the common benefit, protection and security of the law.

Because the case is based exclusively on the Vermont Constitution, there is no further appeal, and the federal and state Defense of Marriage laws will not apply in Vermont at least. The reasoning of the Court is worth noting in this case. The Court began by setting aside the obvious moral, religious, and political implications of the case. In an extensive review of Vermont's 'Common Benefit Clause,' it argued that marriage and its benefits 'enhance the quality of life in our society,' so much so that the basis for not extending them must be strong.

7. "No room at the inn"

During the Christmas season in 2000, I wondered what is the church's appropriate role in society? To lead or to follow?

by Reg Olson, December, 2000

Long ago, we are told, a family in a strange land experienced rejection in their time of need. The woman was decidedly pregnant, and her husband feared that they would have to sleep in the streets, for lack of any accommodations. One inn-keeper, however, showed mercy on the family and offered them the use of his barn.

We wonder why they couldn't find any vacant rooms at the other shelters. Was it because there really was 'no room?' Or was it because they lacked the money to pay the price for a scarce resource? Or was it because they were 'foreigners,' who 'didn't belong here'?

Do we turn out those who seek acceptance and comfort today? The homeless who look for shelter? The refugee in the United States who seeks asylum from Latin America, or the family in Germany, fleeing from the Middle East? What of the former drug addicts or ex-cons who are looking for a job in a tough job-market? And what of the single mother, or the homosexual young person whom we turn away. Are they 'bad role models?' We have become callous to people who don't live up to our standards.

Yet the inn-keeper with the barn shows hospitality to the family whom many today call 'holy.' Similarly the Creator opens his door to all who knock. Can we do any less, especially in this holiday season?

Part VI. WHERE ARE WE GOING?

Overcoming the Barriers of Aimlessness and Powerlessness

"Whither Thou Goest ..."
(Ruth 1:16c KJV)

by Reg and Barbara

THE NARRATIVE

When we began writing this book we felt we were at the point of exasperation. We saw few signs that the problem of homophobia was changing, and that social justice would prevail. Since then we have both retired from our jobs and have gotten involved in various activities which give us reason to be more hopeful. Two of our daughters, Rachel and Liz have continued their involvement in the life of the church. It is not the United Methodist church, but the United Church of Christ which has opened its doors to them. It is ironic that the church which has so boldly proclaimed its motto to be "Open Minds, Open Hearts, Open Doors" should be so rigid on the matter of exclusivity.

At the June, 2002 meeting of the West Ohio Annual Conference of the United Methodist Church I (Reg) retired. This new status gave me a feeling of liberation, for no longer did I fear the possibility that the conference might take away its funding of the Christian Center where I was the executive director, if someone objected to anything which I might have said about homophobia. This liberation gave me the power to speak at annual conference. The group had heard an impassioned plea for the church to be reconciled to its Native American children. Then I said to the entire conference that I found it pleasing for the church to have repented of its complicity with racism (at the general conference in Cleveland, 2000). I also said it was encouraging that the church was reconsidering its relationship to Native Americans. (Why does the church move so slowly?) I then challenged the church to avoid the necessity that sometime in the distant future it might have to repent of its complicity with homophobia. "Let us now open our doors to these children and their families whom we have alienated," I said. A few people applauded this speech, and many others groaned and said, "Not THAT issue again!"

At the end of the annual conference the gathered throng assembled for the ordination of several candidates for ministry. The bishop opened the service with an appeal to give witness to the spirit of God in our presence. He said to the ordinands, "You did not *choose* to become clergy. The Board of Ordained Ministry did not choose you. But *God chose you* and moved you toward this moment of affirmation." At that moment both of us felt intensely sad and angry that the Board and others had indeed *chosen to prevent* many talented people from becoming ordained, people who were *chosen by God* for ministry. We walked out of the service, not able to continue in a worshipful attitude.

Fortunately, our energies have been able to bear fruit in another arena. We were proud to have been co-founders of the Brighton Area PFLAG chapter. In 2002 the chapter received two grants to do programming on Safe Schools. We threw ourselves into this project and provided In-Service training to over 100 teachers in the area's school system, and had public meetings to challenge community residents to make the schools safer for all children. No longer can we allow bullying and intimidation to occur against homosexuals, handicapped children, and those who are members of other racial or ethnic minorities. That kind of bullying had had disastrous results at the Columbine high school in Colorado, and elsewhere.

The community responded in a supportive way to this initiative, and the national PFLAG organization selected the Brighton chapter of PFLAG to receive an award for its efforts. We both were invited to make presentations at the national PFLAG conference and were buoyed up by the countless supporters of PFLAG. Even the picketing of the Fred Phelps people who had heard that Matthew Shepard's mother, Judy, would be there, did not spoil our experience.

It was fulfilling to meet with the United Methodist parents who attended the conference and gathered as a Reconciling Parents Network. We felt that there was a future for the "Open Doors" movement in our church.

Recently we joined the congregation of the Clifton United Methodist Church in Cincinnati, Ohio, one of seven reconciling United Methodist congregations in all of the state of Ohio. More United Methodists live in Ohio than any other state!

What else can we do? We need to speak up when someone makes homophobic slurs in social gatherings. We need to challenge Progressive organizations to be more "gay friendly." We can use humor whenever it can help us in the struggle. The "Heterosexual Questionnaire", found in Appendix 3, is an example of the ironic humor we can use. Most of all, we need to promote serious dialogue and exchange on the subjects of homosexuality and homophobia whenever possible.

We pray that we may go through this struggle with a sense of solidarity with others.

THE DOCUMENTS

1. Barbara's eulogy for her mom's memorial service

When the family gathered for the memorial service of Barbara's mother, her children were encouraged to say a word of remembrance about their mother's life.

by Barbara, May, 30, 2002

This is my second separation from my mother. I actually shed more tears ten years ago. The occasion was the fiftieth anniversary of Mom and Dad, and was celebrated right here in this church. The family gathered, but two of my daughters were banned from the Shram home by my Dad. We realized that Liz and Rachel were created by God as lesbians, but Dad was certain that he could order them to change. Our bags were packed to come for the anniversary, and we prayed for Dad's will to change on this matter, but it didn't happen, not for four years.

Mother was literally caught in the middle, as we supported our daughter and felt unwelcome here as well. We communicated regularly with mother and she struggled for reconciliation. Finally, after four years of turmoil, and Dad's failing health, Mom said to him, 'What is being accomplished by banning Liz and Rachel? Is it okay to invite them to come home?' And Dad said, 'okay.' Who knows what Dad understood at that point? Only God knows! And God released Mother to show love to her eldest granddaughter in person. Some time later, when Rachel's two grandmothers died within a few short weeks of one another, Ramah called her and assured her that Rachel still had one grandmother ... *her*!

Five years ago we were all here for Dad's memorial service and Reg and I are blessed to have our whole family here today from Connecticut, Cincinnati and Dayton. There is a message for our churches in the struggle and reconciliation of Ramah Shram. Christians must become like Ramah and even accept those who are unlike us if we are to truly grasp the unconditional love of God.

2. Jennifer's comments to Barbara after the funeral

Barbara wondered how her comments were received at the funeral. She did not want to antagonize anyone, but she did want to put some things in perspective. Many people indicated that they appreciated the spirit of her comments.

by Jennifer, May, 2002

Mrs. Olson,

Once again, it was wonderful to have the opportunity to meet you, your husband, and many of your beautiful family. I do regret that the circumstances could not have been more joyful. The service was very touching with all the kind words said and references to your mother as an Angel. I saw this card and wanted to share it with you and your family.

I was very moved by your expressions of honest and regretful times, as they affected your daughter, her partner, and your parents. I feel that it is the struggles of a family that strengthen our bonds.

3. Are homosexuals pedophiles?

All too often we hear statements that homosexuals are "dangerous perverts," preying on our children. What are the facts about this allegation?

Summarized by Reg Olson, 2003

Data was gathered from 352 children who were referred to a clinic for evaluation of suspected child sexual abuse. Their mean age was 6.1 years. Subjects' charts were reviewed to examine the relationships of the children to the alleged offender, the sex of the offender, and whether or not the supposed offender was GLBT. After removing subjects who were probably not abused, those who were abused by other children under the age of 18, and cases where the offender's identity was unknown, the researchers examined the remaining subjects. They found that in 82% of the cases the alleged offender was a heterosexual partner of a close relative of the child. Those children who identified the abuser as a recognizable homosexual were from 0% to 3.1%. These figures are within the current estimates of the prevalence of homosexuality in the general community. The authors concluded, "The children in the group studied were unlikely to have been molested by identifiable gay or lesbian people." (From 'Are Children at Risk for Sexual Abuse by Homosexuals?' *Pediatrics* vol. 94, no. 1, July 1994, 41-44, by Carole Jenny, MD, MBA; Thomas A. Roesler, MD; and Kimberly L. Poyer, MSW.)

Research which purports to prove that homosexuals are more likely to be child molesters than heterosexuals fails to live up to accepted methodological standards. They often **assumed** that all male-male molestations were committed by homosexuals. (From website by Gregory M. Herek, Ph.D.)

The percentage of heterosexual Americans who believe the myth that gays and lesbians are child molesters has been *decreasing* from 70% in 1970 to 19% of the men surveyed in 1990 and 10% of women. The proportion of Americans who would allow gay persons to be elementary school teachers was 27% in 1977, and was 54% in 1999.

4. "End this debate"

It is time to stop talking and start conducting direct action, says Soulforce.

by Reg Olson, 2002

In a recent issue of the *Fellowship* magazine Mel White, the executive director of Soul force, Inc., decried the words of an Alabama Southern Baptist Supreme Court Chief Justice, Roy Moore, who said, 'Homosexual practice is a detestable and abominable sin ... by its very nature immoral ... destructive to the natural order of society.' Moore claimed that the 'state has the power to imprison and even execute homosexuals to keep them from influencing children,' (*Fellowship*, May/June, 2002, pages 14-16).

White said that it is time to start a relentless campaign of nonviolent resistance that will cause church leaders to 'do justice at last.' White gave ten reasons to stop participating in 'endless studies and debates' which have allowed anti-gay religious teachings 'to harden into place.' These reasons are:

1. 'By participating in these endless studies and debates, we support our own oppression.' We should no longer give our adversaries a chance to say that homosexuality is a sickness, or a sin.

2. 'By participating we demean ourselves.' He said that the dignity, integrity and right to liberty, life and the pursuit of happiness for the homosexual are not debatable.

3. 'By participating we help cripple the spirits of God's gay children, their friends and families.' Misusing the Bible to condemn homosexuals turns the church into a place of suffering.

4. 'By participating we assume that the decision can be based on scientific or biblical facts.' The church has used biblical literalism and bad science to exclude Gentiles, slaves, people of color, divorcees and LGBT children. This is not a mind issue, but a heart issue, he says.

5. 'By participating we give credibility to the notion that the debate is about homosexuality.' It is really about who has the power to run the church and rule the nation.

6. 'By participating we only confuse further those who haven't made up their minds.' Anti-homosexual

debaters do not listen to serious biblical and mental health arguments, and are not trying to find a compromise position.

7. 'By participating we help maintain a false sense of unity within the Body of Christ. The division is evident, and necessitates ecclesiastical disobedience,' he says.

8. 'By participating we help drive a wedge between us and our gay sisters and brothers.' Why condemn those who are not ready to accept their own homosexuality?

9. 'By participating we help keep the church from doing the work Christ calls it to do.' So many have left the church already over these condemnations.

10. 'By participating we help maintain a heresy that breaks the heart of God.' White notes that, 'God has a special kind of love for the outcast.'

Mel White gives eight suggestions for the next phase of a 'civil rights revolution.' They are:

1. 'Decide that the debate is over ... God loves us without reservation.'

2. 'Oppose, boycott, and protest the studies and debates.'

3. 'Sponsor workshops, seminars, rallies and classes ... and don't allow 'toxic anti-gay misinformation.''

4. 'See ourselves as faithful dissenters,' renewing the church.

5. 'Recruit, train, and organize around the principles of relentless *nonviolent* resistance.'

6. 'We can discontinue our support of clergy, congregations, and denominations who refuse to accept us.'

7. 'Mount permanent protests at church head-quarters and conventions.'

8. 'Mobilize our community now.'

After this 'call to arms' White ends by saying, 'Holly Near wasn't exaggerating when she sang, 'We are a gentle angry people, singing for our lives.'

5. Please help me find the way

When we experience deeply hurt feelings we need someone to talk to. Reg asked his bishop for advice on our struggle.

by Reg, July 1, 2002

Annual Conference 2002

Dear Bishop:

'Could you please help me find the way?' This is a prayer which many drivers utter when faced with changing locations of orange barrels, and lane markers, in the midst of highway repairs and construction projects. It is difficult to know where you are going, especially when you get mixed signals, when some signs are partially covered, and when the path is complicated because of frequent, almost daily, changes. 'It didn't look like this the last time we drove down the road.'

My wife and I had a similar experience at our annual conference this year, because we got mixed signals about where the church was going. We had mixed feelings when we saw the motto for the 2002 West Ohio United Methodist Annual Conference. It was, 'Open hearts, Open Minds, Open Doors.' We certainly appreciate these faith statements. These are good values for a Christian in the twenty-first century. These phrases are used by those who advocate that the church be more open to its various minority members, people of color; people of various ethnic ancestries; and people of different degrees of physical ability, genders, and sexual orientations. 'Open Table,' is the name of one of the groups at our conference. It is comprised of persons who believe that the table to which we are invited (symbolically, the communion table) has been set for *all* of God's children. They say that we should not be exclusive and try to keep certain groups away from the table. When we saw the 'Open hearts, Open Minds, Open Doors' motto we hoped that the Conference was moving in the direction of greater inclusivity. But it soon became apparent that the Conference had not made the progress that we had hoped for. There were no resolutions calling attention to the need to change the church's exclusion of homosexuals. There were very few resolutions that related to any social justice issues. Those which did make it to the agenda were debated by delegates whose views of God ranged, from a God of justice, to a God of private spirituality. Many felt that the Church should not be involved in 'political issues,' except, perhaps, in the issues to which conservative people are committed, such as the anti-lottery movement. At one point the conference was asked to affirm the work and existence of the Board of Church and Society. (It has been under fire from those on the Right who are disturbed by its prophetic witness.) During that debate some speakers said that the Board was biased, supporting those who want the right to have an abortion, and supporting the 'gay life styles,' ordination and marriage of gays. This made us feel uncomfortable, because our own lives have been enriched over the past fifteen years as God created a new awareness in our lives of the need to speak on behalf of those gay, lesbian and transgendered persons who are also persons of faith, but have felt excluded from the church. This exclusion has happened in many denominations, especially in our own United Methodist Church, which has said that homosexual persons are people 'of infinite worth. ...' But this same church has used harsh words of condemnation, saying that homosexuality is contrary to the scriptures.

This has meant that any 'practicing' homosexual cannot be ordained by the church and that people of the same gender, despite their mutual affection and pledges of faithfulness to each other, cannot be united or married in the church. These issues have become very important to us, partly because of friends and members of our own family who have been caught in a confusing web. We and they believe that they are children of God, that they have been given certain gifts and graces, and believe that they had been called upon to serve God, as leaders in the church. But they were told by the church that because of their sexual identity they were not allowed to be ordained.

We are concerned, not only because we have friends and family members who are struggling with this, we also see it as a justice issue. We believe that the struggles for sexual orientation equality are very similar to past struggles for gender and racial equality. At various times the Church has found scriptural texts to suggest that women, homosexuals and African Americans were not worthy, and must be segregated. This was not just an issue of scriptural interpretation, for the church had developed policies to exclude both groups. Traditionally, the church supported slavery, segregation and racism. Even when the three formerly separated Methodist bodies (Methodist Protestant, Methodist Episcopal Church South, and Methodist Episcopal Church, North), came together they tolerated a form of racism. They tried to overcome their political differences on race by a compromise which called for the continuing segregation of African Americans into their own jurisdiction, regardless of their geographical location. It took the Methodist church many years to move beyond that point and abolish the Central Jurisdiction.

It is taking the church a long time to confront the issue of homophobia, which faces us, like an elephant sitting in the living room. Many would prefer to ignore it. 'We can't see it, we can't feel it, we can't smell it, and we can't hear it. It's really not there,' we tell ourselves. This blindness was evident at Annual Conference this year when I made a call for reconciliation. I noted that the conference was fortunate to have a very dramatic presentation by a Native American United Methodist Pastor, who called for reconciliation between Native Americans and European Americans. I said that this was a wonderful thing, and it was too bad that it had taken so long for the church to repent of its complicity with racism, violence and genocide against the Native Americans. I pointed out that similarly, the bishops at the 2000 General Conference in Cleveland had symbolized their repentance for the church's complicity with slavery and racism, in a ceremony involving sack cloth and ashes. Why did it take so long for the church to finally try to cleanse itself of its past sins?

The church moves slowly, and yet our society changes very rapidly. It is as though the church is ambling down a cow path while the society is going full speed ahead on the freeways of the twenty first century. The Church is not leading on the issues of gender, racial and sexual orientation equality. Many businesses, corporations, and institutions of medicine and higher education have gone on record saying that people who are in a same sex relationship should be treated with respect and that they should be given all of the legal privileges of those who are in a heterosexual relationship. But the church seems to be oblivious to this issue. I said to Annual Conference that it has taken us too long to become reconciled with the Native Americans and the African Americans. 'Can't we do something to prevent the continuing rejection and condemnation of homosexuals which will make it unnecessary for us to don sack cloth and ashes some time, maybe a hundred years from now, and repent of our 'past' sins of exclusion?' When that speech was made there was a smattering of applause, and various negative murmurings were heard. Some said, 'Oh here we go again.' There were statements of resentment, 'These are not things that we should speak of in the house of God, or at Annual Conference.'

Some who are caught in the midst of traffic on the changing freeways of life are confused because they get mixed signals, like the newly placed orange barrels and changing lane markers. We want to know which way to go! 'Which way, Oh bishop, will you lead us?' 'Which way, Oh Lord God, do you want us to go?' 'Which way, should we, as clergy, head?'

We felt ambivalent as we looked at and listened to those who made homophobic remarks. We wondered to ourselves, 'Are they really Christian?' Of course they are Christian. They are trying to be Christians. They are people who have come from a Christian tradition. But, as they continue to exclude other members of *our* family, it was so hard to recognize that even they too are our brothers and sisters.

It is so hard to resist the temptation to speak an unkind word or to express resentment as we are confronted by homophobia, racism, sexism and classism which continue in both church and society!

But we made it through Annual Conference and looked forward to the last ceremony, a service which tends to bind United Methodists together, the Ordination Service on Sunday. It is a service which symbolizes new beginnings, just like new lanes or new highways that are open to 'heavenly' traffic. We celebrate the fact that God works among us a great 'traffic controller,' enabling us to find new ways to go, and gives energies to our new Christian leadership. This Service was particularly meaningful for us, because this year I went through the retirement service, having completed thirty-seven years of ministry. This is a transitional ceremony which is always so exciting, as some persons are memorialized, others retire and still others are received into positions of church leadership through ordination to ministry.

We approached this service with high expectations. The auditorium was packed. There was great pageantry, stirring music, beautiful banners, and wonderful robes on display. We were urged to remember the great symbols of the church 'Blessed are the Peacemakers,' 'In Christ there is no East or West,' and, 'We are saved by grace through faith alone.'

Then as the speakers began to lead us into this great ordination experience, they spoke of our baptism. The bishop said that the first ordination was our baptism into the church. 'Remember your baptism and be faithful,' he said. We could not help but recognize that there are so many people who do not take the congregational baptismal vows as seriously as they should. For in baptism we say that we trust what God is doing and that we are grateful that God has shown God's grace to accept the lives of these persons, these lives that we will cherish. But what happens to that respect for these lives if and when these persons grow up and later reveal that they are homosexuals? Many believe that they were made by God to be homosexuals, that it was not an act of choice, for who in their right mind would make such a choice to be ostracized by church and society? Their only choice was to admit their true identity to themselves, and perhaps to the world, if they dared. It was difficult for us, as they spoke of 'remembering our baptism.'

After we had heard the scriptures about being saved by grace alone, the bishop began to preach. And the bishop said that these ordinands did not choose ministry, but were chosen by God. These ordinands were not chosen by the Board of Ordained Ministry, although they had a hand in the proceedings. They had been chosen through the grace of God for ministry. Our hearts fell, as we remembered our own daughter in law, who had wanted to be a Methodist minister since the age of eight, who had graduated from one of the nation's top Methodist seminaries, and who had accomplished so much as she aspired to be a pastor. But she was told by her church, our church, the United Methodist Church, that somehow she had selected herself OUT of the ministry because she was a 'practicing' homosexual. Somehow God's grace was not involved in all of this. She was *outside* of God's grace, and somehow she was not worthy to be ordained in our church!

We did not want to detract from the wonders experienced by others in that auditorium, the music, pageantry and words of the bishop. It is wonderful to see God's grace at work in that way. But we ourselves were overcome with feelings of sadness and exclusion. The road we were traveling seemed to be flanked with barricades and dead-ends. So we quietly excused ourselves from that service and walked out, not in protest, but in sadness. As we silently walked down the street, our eyes fell upon a sign in a store window which read, ***'Sorry, We Are Closed.'*** 'Yes,' we thought, 'we are sorry that the church, and the conference which proclaimed to have 'Open Hearts, Open Minds, and Open Doors' was *closed* to some of God's children.'

We receive mixed messages about baptism, about ordination, and about God's grace. Perhaps mixed messages are better than having no message at all, or having a totally negative message, wherein a unified church might exclude all homosexuals and perhaps persecute them, even as so many were persecuted and killed during the ancient history of the church because they were called 'witches.' Perhaps a mixed message, suggesting that some within the Church understand and are open, even though others in the church may be confused, uncertain and searching, is preferable.

We were fortunate to come upon a fellow pastor, Susan, a woman with whom I had worked on one of the boards of the church. She had not attended the ordination service, and I really believe that God had a hand in her being present, outside the auditorium, as we walked by in our sullenness and grief. We called out to her, greeted her, and said that we needed a pastor. We shared our story, and our concern. She cried with us and prayed with us, thanks be to God.

We receive mixed messages, mixed signals. Some speak with great compassion about the failure of the church to include all God's children, and some others speak with equally great passion against those whom they believe are demons within their midst. Today we ask, in the midst of this situation of contrasting signals, 'What is the road for us, for the Church, for United Methodism, and for our Annual Conference? Show us the way, for we need to know where we are going.'

6. The Clifton United Methodist church

"Of course everyone is welcome in our church. We don't have any signs telling someone to stay away!" Some churches seem to believe that it is obvious that they are open to all persons, others are intentional about declaring their openness.

From the Clifton Church bulletin

"We seek to support, encourage, and empower the ministry of every person, as each of us, in our own way, serves Jesus Christ through the gathered community of faith and through life in the world."

Welcoming Statement

"We, the people of Clifton United Methodist Church, believe that God's love is expansive and unconditional and that through Christ, God has called us to love one another as God loves us. We welcome all people, regardless of gender, race, age, culture, ethnic background, sexual orientation, economic circumstances, family configuration, or difference of faith perspective. We celebrate the worth, dignity and gifts of every person as a child of God."

Epilogue WHAT DOES THE FUTURE HOLD?

Overcoming the Barriers of Impatience and Lack of Trust in God.

"Then I saw a New Heaven and a New Earth . . . for the Former Things Were Passed Away."
(Rev. 21: 1a, 4e RSV)

by Reg and Barbara

THE NARRATIVE

As human beings, we have been blessed with the ability to not only *think* about the future, but to make plans for *shaping* the future. While other creatures of God's world seem to try to prepare for the future, like squirrels burying nuts for future consumption, they often forget what those plans were and are unable to efficiently marshal their energies to effectively survive. Not only do God's children have the ability to shape the future, they have a sense that this action is imperative.

We all talk a lot about making the world "better for future generations." Sometimes we are impatient, as we look for the keys to build a better tomorrow. In this impatience we draft blueprints for a better world, and we express righteous indignation when others seem to stand in the way of progress, "our progress." Sometimes we are exasperated and think that nothing will change and improve. However, the Summer of 2003 brought many events that contributed to our hope and concern.

We live in exciting times, times of struggle and change. In the June, 2003 ruling "Lawrence et al versus Texas," the United States Supreme Court overthrew the so-called "anti-sodomy" law of Texas. In a 6-3 decision the

Court said that the government should not interfere in our private sexual conduct. This action marked the rejection of laws designed to prevent homosexuals from carrying out acts of sexual intimacy. It reversed the court's 1986 ruling which had upheld the Texas statute. Various public opinion polls illustrate changing public sentiment on this issue. In 1986 only 33% of those responding to a Gallup poll supported legalization of homosexual relations between consenting adults. In 1996 that number rose to 44%, and in 2003 it was 60%.

In July, 2003 the Episcopal Church confirmed the election of the first openly gay bishop. The Reverend Canon V. Gene Robinson was elected to his seat in the Diocese of the state of New Hampshire. Last minute attempts by conservative forces to foil his election were defeated.

Some observers believe that the next step will be to legalize marriages for gay persons. In July 2003 the delegates at the national assembly of the Uniting Church in Australia voted to accept gay and lesbian clergy living in committed same sex relationships. In the Canadian Diocese of New Westminster the church has given its blessing to a same sex union.

In November, 2003, Massachusetts became the first State in the nation to grant same sex couples the right to a civil marriage. This will allow same sex couples to visit each other in the hospital without question, to make health care and financial decisions for each other, file joint state tax returns and receive many other protections under state law.

In the United States public support for homosexual marriage has gradually grown over the past few years. A national poll conducted by the Pew Research Center found 65% opposing and 27% supporting gay marriage in 1996. In 2003 it found only 53% opposing and 35% supporting gay unions.

Predictably, conservative religious and political leaders have voiced their opposition to this. Evangelical leaders within the Anglican communion have threatened to divide the church over the issue of a gay priesthood. The Vatican circulated a world wide directive to all priests in 2003, calling them to oppose any government's legalizing of same-sex marriage. It said that homosexual unions are contrary to the Bible and "natural moral law." George W. Bush, the president of the United States, went on record supporting a constitutional amendment called "The Defense of Marriage Act" which would ban same-sex marriage.

We who feel strongly about the rights of homosexuals are caught up in a struggle which polarizes both the church and the state. We believe that God does not follow the public opinion polls, but, God is concerned with ultimate justice. People are tempted to equate their own goals with God's, regardless of which "side" they take on the issue. Should we think that if we don't accomplish OUR goal NOW it won't get done? If same-sex marriage is banned, and if the divisions over homosexuality in the churches cause organizational schism, should we give up and surrender? Should we conclude that our efforts are too insignificant to have an impact on the church or the state, and passively leave the future in God's hands?

Perhaps we need to pause and remember that "God's time is not our time." God's schedule of events may operate in a broader time frame than ours. Although we may be God's instruments, the divine plan unfolds at a time and place known only to the Lord. God does act in loving kindness, but God's precise plans for inclusion of all in the great human family are not clearly known by us.

Let us not forget that the God of creation is still among us, shaping, redeeming, comforting and guarding God's children. God uses us as instruments to spread the good news that we are all God's children, but, God uses other instruments too. The mass media; the government;

secular organizations like PFLAG; and even the Ford Motors Company and American Airlines, which are supporters of PFLAG, may all be instruments in the hands of God. We believe that **God is at work, both outside and inside of the Church!** If freedom and justice for all persons, regardless of sexual orientation, is the purpose of God, it will not be thwarted in the grand scheme of things. We believe that nothing can separate us from the power and love of God. We pray for a New World indeed.

THE DOCUMENTS

1. What has to happen for the church and society to move away from its homophobia?

We wonder what the future holds as we deal with this issue of social injustice.

by Reg Olson, March 16, 2002

Last night we watched commentator Diane Sawyer's interview of celebrity Rosie O'Donnell on network television. The show was entitled 'Rosie's Children.' The show treated a situation in the state of Florida where a gay family of two men and five foster children was fighting for the right to adopt one of the children. State law allows gay families to serve as foster parents, but does not allow gays to adopt children. The featured family had nursed all the children through their condition of being HIV Positive. The fathers were both certified nurses. Theirs was a poignant story. The commentator introduced the show saying that this is not a story about homosexuality, but a show about children in need. Comedienne Rosie O' Donnell came out before a national audience, and announced that she had decided to champion the cause of this family. How ironic, she said, that Florida allowed the family to do the hard work of nursing the children back to health, but would not allow them to adopt the children. Numerous other individuals who were interviewed described the revolving door of foster care. Children recounted being in five to a dozen different foster homes, all the while looking for 'a family that really cared.'

This was not a story about homosexuality? I thought it was. But it was also a story about a group of persons who are being hurt because of our legal system. We were told that Florida alone has thousands of children waiting to be adopted. There are many fit gay parents who would take these children, but are denied that opportunity. Children, and even adults, are being *hurt*.

As I considered the message of this program the thought occurred to me that this principle of focusing on the pain inflicted on people may be an effective way to evoke sympathy. Perhaps those 'dyed in the wool' homophobes would not react in sympathy, but what of the thousands of persons who are undecided as to the proper way to deal with homosexuals? Would this 'Rosie's Children' show and 'crusade' have a positive effect?

Thinking back to the civil rights movement for racial equality, which seems to offer parallels to the movement for gay rights, despite the resistance of many African Americans to this analogy, I tried to remember key events which were turning points in the movement. I remembered the television coverage of mobs of police beating African Americans to their knees, and turning water hoses on them to knock them down in the street. I thought of the scenes of peaceful marchers praying for social justice, only to be faced with more police brutality. People were being hurt.

I thought of the widely acclaimed social psychological research which showed that African American children had a negative self image, due to having internalized the standards of a racist society. Why should a black girl prefer to play with a white doll than a black doll? These children were being hurt.

And my mind turned to the terrible images of Dr. Martin Luther King Jr., whose 'I have a dream' speech I personally heard at the Lincoln memorial in Washington D.C., being savagely shot down by an assassin in Memphis, Tennessee. This man of God was hurt, destroyed!

I think these images and those of the Oxford, Mississippi civil rights workers Andrew Goodman, Michael Schwerner and James Chaney being murdered, the three little black girls killed in a church bombing, and countless lynchings DID help to galvanize sympathy of those who had been 'in the middle of the road' on the race issue. We cannot tolerate people hurting other people, at least publicly!

The stories of the suffering of the supporters of Mahatma Gandhi on his great Salt March had a similar effect. As portrayed in the classic film *Gandhi,* the scores of demonstrators who were beaten to submission by authorities did not suffer in vain. Their hurt aroused others to join in their cause.

Even the sentiment about the American war in Vietnam was affected by a graphic portrayal of human suffering. When the South Vietnamese Colonel's execution of a suspected Viet Cong was featured on the cover of *Newsweek Magazine* people were shocked. When a totally naked little Vietnamese girl was shown fleeing down the street people were shocked. We don't want others to be *hurt*, even if we don't know them, or their cause.

I believe that there are some rumblings in the churches, especially the Presbyterian and United Methodist denominations, of people who are regretting the *hurt* their public statements about homosexuals have caused. I hear pastors say that we have to refrain from homophobic rhetoric, as it may cause discomfort for parishioners who have homosexual members of their families. I read many accounts of interviews of the perpetrators of hate crimes against gay people where the criminal said that he or she was influenced by their preacher, or some public evangelist's diatribes against homosexuals. When confronted, many of these homophobic clergy say that it is not their *intention to hurt* gay people. But this is the result!

A few years ago fifteen United Methodist Bishops broke ranks with the majority of church leaders who defended the United Methodist's rejection of homosexuality. I understand that the motivation for some of these bishops was a realization of the pain, suffering and hurt that some of their colleagues—other bishops, clergy and laity—who had homosexual children and relatives were experiencing as a result of the church's homophobic position.

We must be in solidarity with those who are being hurt. Even the physician's Hippocratic oath says that a doctor should *do no harm.* Can we as Christians do any less? Perhaps it doesn't matter if you think that gay families will cause their children to become gay (a position refuted by reputable research). Perhaps it doesn't matter if we accept the stereotypes of gay people as having a 'gay agenda.' Perhaps it doesn't matter if we know, or *like* any gay people. It **does matter** to many, even in the 'silent majority,' that people are being *hurt* by our social policies in Florida, in the United Methodist and Presbyterian churches, and in our society. Let us vow to 'do no harm.'

2. Dare to be Christian

Why are we always being apologetic about our beliefs? Why do we allow our opponents take the so called "high ground" in their discussion of homosexuality?

by Reg Olson, January, 2003

1. Nowhere in God's law of the **Ten Commandments** does it say that God hates homosexuals.

How dare **we** reject them?

2. Nowhere in the **Gospels** does Christ say we should hate homosexuals.

How dare **we call** them sinners?

3. In our congregational vows at a **baptism, we covenant** with the infant and their family to help raise and support them.

How dare **we turn them out** them if later they come out gay?

4. The United Methodist Church has declared that it practices **"Radical Hospitality."**

How dare **we be inhospitable** to gays as the men of Sodom were inhospitable to the guests of Lot?

5. The United Methodist Church has declared that it practices **'Risk Taking.'**

How dare it **take a passive attitude** about discussing the challenge of homosexuality to the church? ("Oh no, not that subject again!")

6. A homophobic society spreads false **stereotypes**, saying **that most homosexuals are child molesters**, while it is proven that heterosexuals are far more prone to be pedophiles.

How dare United Methodists **spread this falsehood**?

7. The church claims to uphold **family values**, yet it disallows the marriage of committed members of the same-sex and forces them into 'illicit' relationships.

How dare we **prevent couples** from entering a 'family relationship?'

8. Society spreads false **stereotypes** saying **that homosexuals are promiscuous**.

How dare we do so, when, **in truth**, committed lesbian partners have the most faithful relationships, exceeding the longevity of heterosexual partnerships ?

9. The Church says that it recognizes the **Call of God to ministry**.

How dare **we exclude** from ministry those persons called by God to ministry?

10. The Church says it practices **forgiveness** for sinners. How dare it **focus on homosexuality** as the supposed 'ultimate' sin when God gives us the gift of sexuality?

11. The Bible speaks of **rejection of the Holy Spirit** as the 'unforgivable sin.' How dare we r**eject the work** of the Holy Spirit in lives of countless Christian homosexuals who have been forced to leave an inhospitable church in numbers estimated to equal those of the Hebrew Exodus? (600,000, according to a recent estimate).

12. The Church claims to practice **unconditional love**.

How dare it **rebuff loving** homosexuals and offer to accept them only if they 'convert' to heterosexuality?

13. The Church claims to **oppose violence** and hate crimes in our society.

How dare it **foster a hatred** of homosexuals which a majority of the perpetrators of hate crimes against homosexuals say they **learned in the church**?

14. The Church says it **appreciates diversity**, for God has created us all to be to be different in some way.

How dare it **exclude** a whole group because it has a different sexual orientation?

15. The Church proclaims it is here to **save sinners**.

How dare the church **turn a blind eye** to one of the greatest sins of our time, namely **OUR REJECTION** of homosexual persons and condemnation of many young people to hopelessness and suicide?

16. The Church proclaims the equality of all persons in the eyes of God.

How dare we elevate a message of **MALE DOMINANCE** which ultimately **undergirds** our homophobia?

17. The Church **Must Cleanse Itself** from the sin of homophobia, for **God dares to forgive it**, if it truly repents.

18. The **Church has**, of late, **repented** of the past sins of racism and violence against Native Americans and Blacks.

It is time to **repent of homophobia**, and not 'sin, that grace may abound.'

3. From the sin of exclusion to the practice of inclusion, one stone at a time

A partial answer to our question, "How Long, O Lord?" is that it depends on how long we remain unaware of the sinfulness of exclusion.

by Reg Olson, 2000

Have you ever heard that some animal species eat their young? This revelation is appalling to one who believes in the 'sanctity of the family.' But, animals are just that—animals! The basic difference between 'higher forms of life,' namely human life, and that of 'lower animal forms' may be whether or not humans have attained the image of God. A fundamental difference between the baser animalistic tendencies and those of truly human beings is whether they are inclusive or exclusive in their intra-specific relationships.

The inclusion of others can be expanded to include an increasing number of categories of people. At the elementary levels we must decide if we accept or reject members of our family. Do we really love our parents? Our brothers and sisters? Our aunts and uncles? Our close cousins? Our distant cousins? Conservatives like to proclaim the value of familial love. Indeed, the ability to love others, beyond oneself is a mark of civility.

Can we also love others in our *village*, who may not be relatives? What of those of other body types—weight, height, gender, or handicap? What of those whose status is different from ours? Those having less education, less prestigious occupations, whose age is greater than ours, and whose sexual orientation is different from ours? What of those who speak a different language, have a different religion, and live in another nation?

Sociologists use the term 'reference groups' to indicate a standard by which we judge ourselves, in comparison to others. The reference group enables persons to define how well they are doing. A wealthy person may compare herself to another wealthy person 'keeping up with the Joneses'. A person of moderate income may compare himself to one who is in poverty, and feel superior in the process. It seems handy to have others of lower status to be our negative referents ('thank God we are not like them,' we say.) We seem to want scapegoats who can be recipients of our negative judgments. In our youth, many of us experienced the humiliation of being rejected (or chosen last) in playground activities during the 'choosing up of sides' for a game of kickball, or baseball. As adults we want to be on the 'chosen' side.

Exclusion has many forms. There is a continuum between inclusion and exclusion. Full inclusion of another involves embracing them as equals, while full exclusion is related to the possibility of murdering others. There are several intermediate attitudes between the extremes, such as the following:

INCLUSION (which is GODLY)
Embracing others as equals
Protecting others
Acceptance of differences
Tolerance of differences
Discomfort with differences
Rejection of others
Persecution of others
Elimination of others
EXCLUSION (which is BASE)

We may reject others because of their status, or their behavior. We may also impute certain behaviors to those who are different, such as allegations about their mental abilities, their sexual behavior, their 'criminal' behaviors, etc. Exclusion may be subtle, such as telling or believing stereotypes about others. The biblical writer of John's letters called attention to the inappropriateness of exclusion when he wrote, 'How can you say that you love God, whom you have not seen, when you do not love mankind, whom you have seen?'

In its extreme form, exclusion amounts to the denial of another person's humanity. When this is done the taking of that person's life is easier. In a war we prepare to do battle with the 'Hun,' the 'Jap,' the 'Communist,' the 'Cong.' Similarly, we define others as being inferior when we use epithets and refer to them as 'Kike,' 'Wop,' Pollock," and 'Chink.'

During the past thirty years the United Methodist Church has not appeared to be too 'gay-friendly.' It has not allowed homosexuals to become clergy, or to be united in matrimony. But the *United Methodist Discipline*, in its statement that 'homosexuals are persons of sacred worth' has, in my opinion, at least prevented us from overtly persecuting gays and lesbians. Yet homosexuals are one of the last groups of human beings to be included in the 'family of God.'

A demonstration of our growing civility (those uncomfortable with this call it being PC, 'politically correct') is seen in our acceptance of others who are deemed to be different from us. Does God really **LOVE** people who are short, overweight, handicapped, illiterate, old, homosexual, non-Christian, non-white, and non-English-speaking? **Of course God does! Do we**? Another important question is, 'Whom does God favor?' Sometimes we seem to think that the more people are like us the more they are loved by God (who also is like us). This is called ethnocentrism. This is like asking a parent, 'which of your children do you love the most?' When my grandmother was asked that question she showed the questioner her hand and asked, 'which finger do I love the most?' The answer was, of course, that all digits are indispensable!

There are varying degrees of inclusivity. Can we allow another to survive? To be a citizen of our country? To reside in our neighborhood? To work in our workplace? To have legal rights and protections? To go to our school? To marry others like themselves? To marry into our family? To allow our child to come out of the closet and choose a life partner?

The church has the moral responsibility to help its members and our society expand their range of acceptance of others who are dissimilar to themselves. This is the true attainment of the image of God, 'loving your neighbor as yourself.'

Retired Methodist bishop of South Africa, Peter Story once preached about three soldiers on the battlefields of World War I. When one was shot and killed by the enemy, his two comrades took his body to a nearby village in Belgium and sought the help of the parish priest in giving their friend a Christian burial. The priest asked if the fallen solder had been a Protestant or a Catholic. The soldiers said they didn't know, but didn't think he was Catholic. The priest responded by saying that non-Catholics could not be buried within the hallowed, consecrated ground of the church graveyard, but he would help them bury the soldier outside the walled cemetery. Quietly they did their work, and fashioned a simple wooden cross as a marker for the grave. As the two soldiers returned to their unit they pondered about the church which did not have room for their comrade in arms. 'What kind of a church and what kind of a God treats people as second class citizens?,' they wondered. The next day the soldiers returned with flowers for the grave, but they could not find their friend's gravesite with the freshly made cross. After a diligent search, they discovered that a portion of the cemetery's stone wall now jutted out beyond its former boundaries. Just inside this irregularity of the boundary they found the new grave! It seemed that the priest had agonized about his exclusionary decision, and had spent most of the night expanding the cemetery, by single handedly moving the wall, one stone at a time! This is truly the action of a God of inclusive love. It may not be easy for us to imitate God, but how can we try to do anything less?

4. Canada survives gay marriage ruling

What might happen to society if it becomes truly open to homosexuals? Should religious people listen to the views of representatives of a secular society when they share their observations about religion? Read this and decide for yourself.

by Tony Brown, theater critic of *The Plain Dealer.* He was on assignment in Canada. July 5, 2003

Stratford, Ontario - I've been in Canada for more than a week, and so far I haven't seen any thunderbolts striking our neighbors to the north dead. Traditional Canadian married couples, husband and wife, can be seen walking along together just as before. Traditional Canadian families — mom, pop and the kids — have not suddenly disintegrated.

I happened to bicycle by an outdoor chapel and witnessed three sets of June brides and June grooms taking their vows, and at my hotel I spied a sign advertising the 50th wedding anniversary of an elderly man and woman.

Ontario has legalized gay marriage, and nothing about the country appears to have been consumed by hellfire and brimstone. None of the dire consequences predicted by conservative groups in the United States should our country welcome gays and lesbians into the blissful state of matrimony seem to have materialized here.

What we call the family unit has not been destroyed. The sacrament of marriage remains unbesmirched. The wrath of God has not been visited upon anyone in particular.

There are other signs that the far right may be all wrong about the gay issue in the United States as well.

The Supreme Court finally struck down the Texas sodomy law last week. An actual gay couple (not a fictional one on a sitcom) shared a passionate kiss on the nationally televised Tony Awards a couple of weeks ago after winning the prize for writing the score of 'Hairspray.' CBS got 10 phone calls and 68 e-mails from 8 million viewers. Not only that, but the best actor in a musical Tony award went to a gay man who wears a dress and plays a woman in 'Hairspray.' And the best-play award went to 'Take Me Out,' a show about a star baseball player who comes out of the closet. Ramifications: none. Attendance jumped at both award-winning shows after the broadcast.

Meanwhile, Episcopalians in New Hampshire recently elected the first openly gay bishop in the worldwide

Anglican communion. I belong to an Episcopal church in Cleveland, Trinity Cathedral, which I have attended several times since this happy news broke, and no one has bolted the place. If anything, it feels even more inclusive than before. I wouldn't be surprised to learn that we picked up a few new members who feel more at home in a church that welcomes everyone.

We in Cleveland seem to have taken many strides of late to be more inclusive. The dean of my church, the Very Rev. Tracey Lind, is a lesbian. In her nearly three years there, Trinity has expanded and prospered, not so much because of her sexual orientation but because she is a fine preacher and urban activist. In Cleveland Heights, city workers who are gay can now share their workplace benefits with their live-in lovers, thanks to a city ordinance. That eastern suburb is also home to a recent petition effort that will bring to the ballot a proposal to officially recognize all such non-marital unions. And across town in Lakewood earlier this month, Mayor Madeline Cain stood her ground and let the rainbow flag of inclusion fly at city hall during Gay Pride Week.

The result of all this gay-rights activity in Canada, in the United States, in the Episcopal Church and in Cleveland has not been the diminishment of rights for non-gays that conservatives have predicted.

I'm a straight, white, married male, and I feel nothing but joy in being able to commune more closely with my gay brothers and sisters, to celebrate being alive on the planet with them.

Of course, many conservatives say that my punishment, and the punishment of those who think like me, awaits the Judgment Day, when God's wrath will be unmerciful.

As colorful as this image may be, it is a twisted reading of scripture. While the Old Testament's Book of Leviticus condemns homosexuality, it also proscribes wearing clothes made of two fabrics (forget those polyester blends), eating raw meat (carpaccio is out) and touching the skin of a dead pig (rendering football sinful).

Nowhere in the Gospels, on the other hand, does Jesus say anything one way or the other about homosexuality. But he does say, repeatedly, that it is good to embrace those who are different from us, repel us and offend us. Even those who wear polyester blends.

According to surveys, Canadians are far less likely than Americans to identify themselves as church going Christians. Which brings up this ticklish question: Why are the Canadians, who increasingly say they have given up the church, behaving in a much more Christ-like manner than many so-called 'Christian conservatives' in America?

If that question lands me in hell, so be it. For the time being, I'm in the other place. I'm in Canada.

5. How long oh Lord?

When the General Conference of the United Methodist Church donned sack cloth and ashes to repent for the church's former support of slavery I thought that this act was a little late, maybe 150 years late. We wondered how long before the church would repent of its homophobia.

by Reg Olson, 2001

The year was 2124. Americans had built their second space station on Mars. The Chinese had constructed a Venus orbiting station. Scientists vowed to conquer Cerebral Palsy just as they had successfully eliminated Cancer and Heart Disease. Bishop David Justice, an openly gay clergyman who had been in a committed gay relationship of 30 years officiated at the reunification service in Philadelphia. He and his clergy partner had been one of the first gay clergy couples to share an appointment to a local church. A lot had changed in Methodism!

Since the General Conference of 2040 the United Methodist Church had been divided between the 'Reconciling Methodists' and the 'Good News Methodists.' The division had occurred over issues of homosexuality. In 2040 the General Conference of the then united Methodist Church had narrowly passed legislation to depart from its condemnation of homosexuality, same-sex marriages, and ordination of gays, lesbians and transsexuals. The Good News Church had immediately reiterated its statement that homosexuality was 'incompatible with Christian teaching.' It had also passed a requirement that all clergy take a vow not to conduct a same-sex union, and not to 'read any 'gay-friendly' literature that had been inspired by the devil.' To own or carry such writings was deemed a punishable offense. The state had made same-sex marriages legal twenty years earlier. Rumor had it that at Jurisdictional Conference next month five more openly gay bishops would be chosen.

Now in 2124, Bishop David Justice led the conference in a prayer of penitence. He praised God from whom all blessings flow—the blessings of comfort, justice and reconciliation. He confessed the church's past sins of institutional homophobia, and the lack of fortitude of those who had only silently supported inclusiveness for many years.

As he prayed, delegates remembered that an estimated one million persons had joined the church since that infamous day of division. That was perhaps half of those who had been forced out of the church or had voluntarily left because of the church's punitive attitude toward homosexuals and their supporters.

The bishop solemnly thanked God for the rich cloud of witnesses whose lives and commitment had made this day possible—men and women, young and old, black and white, gay and straight persons. He quietly acknowledged the lack of courage of the church in not speaking out against anti-gay violence, and in abdicating its prophetic role.

As he prayed delegates remembered how, when scientists had conclusively proved that sexual orientation was genetically based, many churchmen and women had continued to condemn homosexuals, saying that even alcoholics have to learn to live with their 'infirmities.'

Bishop Justice implored God to reinstate the role of the church on the cutting edge of social justice, rather than being a 'Johnny come lately.' He remembered the lives of those who had died, been murdered, or committed suicide because they were not accepted in the church which had baptized them.

The delegates remembered the massacre of thirteen people in a 'Reconciling Congregation' twelve years ago. It was an act of hatred committed by a church member who said he was cleansing the church of its sin. Justice gave thanks for the lives of committed men and women, gay and straight, who had strengthened the fabric of the family, and upheld the sanctity of marriage, whether between heterosexuals or homosexuals.

Delegates recalled that it had been twenty years since the state had legalized same sex marriages. But many church leaders had said it was not their choice to subscribe to such a 'sinful' union. They also remembered that society had been surprised to learn, after the legalization of same-sex marriages, that the levels of pederasty, sexual assault, and promiscuity had not increased as a result, but that gays in committed relationships were recognized to have greater fidelity than heterosexuals! This marital faithfulness had even increased after state sanctions were lifted and it had become easier to have their relationship supported publicly. The birth rate had not declined as a result of this legislation. And the overall marital stability rate had actually increased as a result of a new wave of faithfulness. Bishop Justice continued, saying, 'O Lord, we remember the words of Bishop Jack Tuell who said in 2000 that, 'God is doing a new thing.' We give you thanks for having revealed your compassion for all and your displeasure with our homophobia. We wonder, why, O God, it has taken so long for the church to listen. Forgive us for our intransigence.'

Historians in the conference remembered the similarities between this historic day and the service of 1939 which had ended eighty years of separation between the northern and southern Methodist Episcopal Churches, a division over slavery and racism. There had been so many parallels between the movements to end racism and heterosexism, the educational efforts, demonstrations, coalition building, nonviolent civil disobedience, assassinations of public figures, social legislation and acts of public repentance.

The bishop gave special thanks to PFLAG, Reconciling United Methodists, and other groups of persons who had stood in support of loved ones who were homosexual. He also showed special gratitude to the fifteen bishops who, long ago in 1996 first made their witness against exclusivity in the church. Recognizing that not all were yet reconciled, the bishop prayed for those who continued to treat women, African Americans, Latinos, and Gays as biologically inferior people who were beyond God's love. 'We pray for them,' he said, 'not in judgment, but in sadness for their obstinacy, and in hopes for their salvation. Grant O Lord, that those who remain outside our fellowship may remember the words, 'why do you think that blowing out another's candle will make yours shine more brightly?' In the name of the Risen Lord, we pray, let the church say— AMEN.'

Some theologians in the conference thought to themselves, 'Well the church has finally changed! It does take a long time.' And the mothers of homosexuals in the convention center thought, 'How Long, O Lord?'

How Long O Lord? Indeed. [8]

6. "God of history—recent, ancient"

One of the hymns sung by the reconciliation group at General Conference affirmed the continuing work of God.

Words by Jane Parker Huber @ 1984, sung to tune Hyfrydol 87 87 D
(tune of "Come Thou Long Expected Jesus")

THE HYMN, "GOD OF HISTORY—RECENT, ANCIENT"

God of history—recent, ancient—
God of every yesterday,
Still our God in this day's moments,
Where we go or where we stay;
You have set us in this context,
Time relationship, and place,
Hear our praise and glad thanksgiving
For all signs of present grace.

You have called us from division
Into unity and hope.
Each and all belong together
In the world's kaleidoscope.
Help us listen to the voices
Daring us to be and do
What you plan for church and people,
Loving others, praising you.

How are we then, called to answer
As we work and as we live.
Called to justice, called to mission,
Learning to receive and give?
Shall we build a bridge of promise?
Tear down walls that split divide?
Fling wide doorways, open windows?
Let the Spirit come inside?

God, you point us toward the future
Where Christ leads and shows the way.
Here and now, work not yet finished
Needs our strength and will today.
Thus we move into tomorrow,
Called to live and work and be
Reconcilers, pilgrim people,
Called by Christ, by Christ set free.

APPENDIX

1. A Chronology of Events Underlying the Correspondence in Part II

by Barbara

My father had had a heart attack shortly after his retirement in 1980. He would also have several strokes, cancer, and, finally, Alzheimer's disease.

Liz and Jim were married in 1985.

Liz came out to her parents in Michigan June, 1988, 2 ½ years after marriage.

The BANNING letter was written and sent December 1991.

We visited my parents at Easter, 1992, with me not knowing about the ban.

My parents' fiftieth anniversary celebration was June 19, 1992.

June 1993 Liz and Rachel moved to Minneapolis.

We did not attend the 1993 reunion.

August, 1993 my sister, Mary "laid into" me for destroying the family, and for Reg's "interference" in family affairs.

My father had some surgery December, 1993.

We visited Brownsburg in January, 1994 after Ramah falsely said Liz could come home.

We attended the family reunion 1994 in hopes of a reconciliation.

January 27, 1995 I wrote "Dear Mother Shram".

My Mom called, to start our reconciliation, in January, 1995.

The extended family had a last communion with Dad at his nursing home, where he had resided only three months, July 25, 1997. Reg officiated at the service.

My father died July 30, 1997.

On August 4, 1997 we had a memorial service for my father, with all the extended family, including Liz and Rachel, present.

2. "But OUR Church Doesn't Reject Homosexuals!"

How can we determine if our church is really friendly or open to gays and lesbians? Reg designed this questionnaire to stimulate discussion and thought.

by Reg, December 14, 2000

'But OUR Church Doesn't Reject Homosexuals!', you say. That's good! But have you seriously considered whether or not our church practices *any* of a variety of forms of discrimination and rejection? Like so much of life, it is not a question of being 100% rejecting or 100% accepting. Here are some questions we might want to ask of ourselves as a congregation to measure the **extent of** our acceptance of homosexual persons: Answer each question in reference to **your congregation**.

For each of the following indicate whether you

Strongly agree with the statement	SA
Just moderately agree	A
Are undecided about the statement	U
Just moderately disagree	D
Strongly disagree with the statement	SD

If you 'don't know' what the answer is leave the item blank.

1. We don't have any homosexuals in our congregation	SA A U D SD
2. Homosexuals in our congregation are 'out of the closet' (open about their sexuality)	SA A U D SD
3. In our congregation homosexuals find that they are not the only gay people here	SA A U D SD

4. Homosexuals generally feel comfortable in our congregation SA A U D SD
   a. Homosexuals generally feel accepted in our congregation SA A U D SD
5. Homosexuals who come to our church are never verbally abused here SA A U D SD
   a. Homosexuals who come to our church are never verbally abused (anywhere) SA A U D SD
6. Homosexuals who come to our church are never physically abused here SA A U D SD
   a. Homosexuals who come to our church are never physically abused (anywhere) SA A U D SD
7. In our church homosexuals are never made to feel uncomfortable if they sit with their partners in services or at meetings SA A U D SD
8. Homosexual couples **should** never show affection toward each other (kiss or hold hands) in our congregation SA A U D SD
   a. Homosexual couples **would** never show affection toward each other (kiss or hold hands) in our congregation SA A U D SD
9. People don't talk about homosexuality in our congregation SA A U D SD
10. Our congregation is grappling with the issue of reconciliation between heterosexuals and homosexuals SA A U D SD
11. In our church meetings we sometimes discuss the 'causes' of homosexuality SA A U D SD
12. We never discuss hate crimes against homosexuals in our church meetings SA A U D SD
13. Our congregation used the United Methodist curriculum to study the issue of homosexuality SA A U D SD
    a. Many church members were involved in that study SA A U D SD
    b. Our congregation does this kind of study every year SA A U D SD

14. Our national and state-wide church conferences practice full openness and inclusion of homosexuals SA A U D SD
15. People in our congregation do not think it is good to be a homosexual SA A U D SD
16. People in our congregation say that the 'practice of homosexuality is not acceptable.' SA A U D SD
17. There are no support groups or resources for homosexuals in our church (literature or PFLAG groups or counseling perceived as supportive) SA A U D SD
18. In our congregation we often try to counsel homosexuals to become heterosexual SA A U D SD
19. We have no restrictions in our congregation against the full participation of homosexuals in the life of the church SA A U D SD
    a. They can join the church SA A U D SD
    b. They can be baptized in the church SA A U D SD
    c. They can take communion SA A U D SD
    d. They can teach Sunday School SA A U D SD
    e. They can direct or participate in the music program SA A U D SD
    f. They can be on our committees SA A U D SD
    g. Their committed relationships can be sanctified SA A U D SD
    h. They can be ordained as clergy SA A U D SD
    i. They can be paid support staff SA A U D SD
    j. They can serve as ministers here SA A U D SD
20. We attempt to expose and challenge negative stereotypes about homosexuals SA A U D SD
21. In our congregation we condemn the use of anti-gay humor SA A U D SD
22. Other people in our congregation seem to feel uncomfortable around homosexuals SA A U D SD
23. Our congregation sees heterosexuality as a gift from God SA A U D SD
    a. Our congregation sees homosexuality as a gift from God SA A U D SD
24. We never debate about homosexuality in

our congregation	SA A U D SD
25. Our town is a safe environment for homosexuals	SA A U D SD
26. Our law enforcement officials don't discriminate against gays	SA A U D SD
27. There are social gathering places for homosexuals in our town	SA A U D SD
28. Any anti-gay hate crimes are taken very seriously in our town and not tolerated	SA A U D SD
29. I think we should learn to feel comfortable talking about homosexuality	SA A U D SD
30. The Bible clearly rejects the practice of homosexuality	SA A U D SD
31. Homosexuals are typically promiscuous	SA A U D SD
32. Homosexuals are usually sexual predators against children	SA A U D SD

3. Heterosexual Questionnaire

Sometimes humor allows us to release some of our tensions. The HETEROSEXUAL QUESTIONNAIRE shows us the ridiculousness of some of our so-called "helpful" approaches toward homosexuals. Unfortunately, the substance of some of these questions is frightfully serious.

by Martin Rochlin, Ph.D., January 2001

1. What do you think caused heterosexuality?
2. When and how did you first decide you were heterosexual?
3. Is it possible your heterosexuality is just a phase you may grow out of?
4. Is it possible your heterosexuality stems from a neurotic fear of others of the same sex?
5. Isn't it possible that all you really need is a good gay lover?

6. Heterosexuals have histories of failures in gay relationships. Do you think you may have turned to heterosexuality out of fear of rejection?

7. If you've never slept with a person of the same-sex, how do you know you wouldn't prefer that?

8. If heterosexuality is normal, why is a disproportionate number of mental patients heterosexual?

9. To whom have you discussed your heterosexual tendencies? How did they react?

10. Your heterosexuality doesn't offend me as long as you don't try to force it on me. Why do you people feel compelled to seduce others into your sexual orientation?

11. If you choose to nurture children, would you want them to be heterosexual, knowing the problems they would face?

12. The great majority of child molesters are heterosexuals. Do you really consider it safe to expose your children to heterosexual teachers?

13. Why do you insist on being so obvious, and making a public spectacle of your heterosexuality? Can't you just be what you are and keep it quiet?

14. How can you ever hope to become a whole person if you limit yourself to a compulsive, exclusive heterosexual objective choice and remain unwilling to explore and develop your normal, natural, healthy, God-given homosexual potential?

15. Heterosexuals are noted for assigning themselves and each other to narrowly restricted stereotyped sex roles. Why do you cling to such unhealthy role-play?

16. Why do heterosexuals place so much emphasis on sex?

17. With all the societal support marriage received, the divorce rate is spiraling. Why are there so few stable relationships among heterosexuals?

18. How could a human race survive if everyone were heterosexual, considering the menace of over population?

19. There seem to be very few happy heterosexuals. Techniques have been developed with which you might be able to change if you really want to. Have you considered aversion therapy?

FOOTNOTES

[1] However, Thomas E. Fank, *Polity, Practice and Mission of the United Methodist Church* 1998 said there is no crisis of decline, but populations shifts and changes in mobility, education levels and birth rate.

[2] A recent study found that churches which leave their doors locked are twice as likely to be robbed as those which are left unlocked. This was true whether they were in urban or rural areas. The crimes included not only theft, but also malicious damage and arson. It is true whether the church was large or small. "Cathedrals don't suffer much from crime because there are always people about," says Brian King, of *Ecclesiastical*, an English insurance company for churches.

The churches which are most inclusive can share their gifts more widely, and not lose them. "If a man lights a candle and puts it under a basket, it will not shed light." (Cedric Pulford, "Open-doors safest bet for churches, say British security groups," *Ecumenical News International,* April 2, 2003, page 23.)

There is a message here for churches in America too. Churches have something precious in them (the Gospel), but it is most accessible in churches which are open to the greater public. The churches which are most exclusive and wish to keep their treasures to themselves are most likely to lose them!

[3] Pastor Van Kuiken was charged with violating the Presbyterian Church's Book of Order in April, 2003. The presbytery ruled that Van Kuiken was guilty of violating church law, and gave him a reprimand. They said that any union he performed between homosexual persons should not be called a "marriage." When he vowed to continue the

practice the Church de-frocked him (June 16, 2003).

Writing in the *Cincinnati Enquirer*, April 15, 2003, Dan Klepal said, " ... some ministries are rebelling against a ruling by the Presbyterian General Assembly's highest court that homosexuals cannot be married within the church. The rule, named "The Benton Rule" after the pastor who brought the complaint against a New York pastor who was performing same-sex marriages in 1991, allows for "holy unions" between homosexual people but says they cannot be considered "marriages."

That smacks of hypocrisy to homosexuals and ministers who say the unions are exactly the same as heterosexual marriages. The ruling also doesn't sit well with the people on the other side of the issue, who believe the church should not condone homosexual unions at all. Marc Benton, pastor of the Bethlehem Church in New York who brought the New York complaint, said the ruling was a political compromise that has done more to divide the church than bring it together. "The ruling was a farce that was trying to appease both sides," Benton said. "They've consistently tried to do that, and the problem is you can't, with this sharp a difference on an issue like this. "Unless these two issues are settled in a way that assures the majority of the church that we're serious about maintaining our historical stand on these things, the church will implode."

4. Ironically, this pastor was later expelled from his denomination because of heterosexual impropriety. He was then replaced by a woman pastor who had a reputation of being supportive of ministry to homosexuals!

5. 162 H Equal Rights Regardless of Sexual Orientation

"Certain basic human rights and civil liberties are due all persons. We are committed to supporting those rights and liberties for homosexual persons. We see a clear issue of simple justice in protecting their rightful claims where they have shared material resources, pensions, guardian relationships, mutual powers of attorney, and other such lawful claims typically attendant to contractual relationships that involve shared contributions, responsibilities, and liabilities, and equal protection before the law. Moreover, we support efforts to stop violence and other forms of coercion against gays and lesbians. We also commit ourselves to social witness against the coercion and marginalization of former homosexuals."

6. 332.6 Unauthorized Conduct
"Ceremonies that celebrate homosexual unions shall not be conducted by our ministers and shall not be conducted in our churches."

7. 304.3 The Ministry
"While persons set apart by the Church for ordained ministry are subject to all the frailties of the human condition and the pressures of society, they are required to maintain the highest standards of holy living in the world. Since the practice of homosexuality is incompatible with Christian teaching, self-avowed practicing homosexuals (1) are not to be accepted as candidates, ordained as ministers, or appointed to serve in The United Methodist Church.

> (1) "Self-avowed practicing homosexual" is understood to mean that a person openly acknowledges to a bishop, district superintendent, district committee of ordained ministry, board of ordained ministry, or clergy session that the person is a practicing homosexual."

8. A recent publication notes that some "conservative renewal groups" have "found a tried and true

wedge issue [homosexuality], that stirs emotions while obscuring the real story" (*United Methodist @ RISK, A Wake-Up Call, by Leon Howell,* Kingston, New York, Information Project for United Methodists, 2003.) The author says, "Mainstream Protestant churches have struggled for 25 years to find a way to affirm that Christian gays and lesbians have a place at the altar. Using the issue to discredit churches and their leadership is reprehensible. Lesbians and gay men are 'persons of sacred worth.' They are not epithets," (*Risk*, pages 77, 78).

PERMISSIONS

The authors are grateful for the permission granted to reprint the following materials:

"A Reconciling Congregation" From a shared e-mail, Monday 9, October 2000 (author unknown)
"Bishop calls for PFLAG Alliance" ©Paul Beeman
"Canada Survives Gay Marriage Ruling" ©Tony Brown, *The Cleveland Plain Dealer*, July 5, 2003, 2003.
"Civil Unions in Vermont!" ©American Anglican Council
"Clifton United Methodist Church Bulletin" Clifton United Methodist Church
"Commentary: Its Time to Re-Imagine Our Relationships," ©United Methodist News Service
"God of History, Recent, Ancient" Words by Jane Parker Huber @ 1984,
"Heterosexual Questionnaire" Martin Rochlin, Ph.D. 1/2001 (unable to locate the original source, received via e-mail)
"Homosexuals and the Holocaust" © Ben S. Austin, holocaust\shoah
"Jack Tuell Took a New Look," ©United Methodist News Service
"Methodists Pull Funds From Group That Accepted Gay Students" ©*Chronicle of Higher Education*
"Phil Hart," ©United Methodist News Service
"Reform Jewish Leaders Approve Same-Sex Unions" Reprinted with permission of the Associated Press
"Statement by Parents Reconciling Network" ©Parents Reconciling Network
"Statement of Clergy Commitment" originally released March 2, 1998, used by permission of Affirmation: United Methodists for Lesbian, Gay, Bisexual, & Transgender Concerns, umaffirm.org.

“The Heresy Trial of Bishop Joseph Sprague,” ©United Methodist News Service

“Two Days of Civil Disobedience,” ©Laura Montgomery Rutt, Director of Communications for Soulforce, Inc.

“When Were You Supposed To Start Hating My Son?” ©PFLAG, by G. Mater (unable to locate the original source, received via e-mail)